Jesus
on the side
of
the Weak

Yongjea John Han

ISBN-13: 978-1-7750387-0-2

CONTENTS

INTRODUCTION

IT IS BORN AS THE SON OF GOD.

THE REGION of Israel where Jesus Christ was active 2000years ago was a political and economic confusion. Politically, the perpetual invasion of the countries around Israel, especially the territory of the Roman imperialism and the impoverishment of the national rights, gave the Israelites a great deal of pain and confusion. During the 430years of the middle ages of Israel and the New Testament, Israel tried to maintain its own religious and political vigor from the Old Testament era. During that period, the anti-imperialist uprising of the people took place, in which the identity of the Jews as the chosen people of God has been preserved in the great religious roots of Judaism. Jesus Christ was born in Bethlehem, Judea, according to the prophecies of the Old Testament about BC4. His appearance became the only way out for the Israelites who had long been thirsty for spiritual hunger and for those seeking political breakthroughs of liberation. As he spent his childhood and boyhood in a small town called Nazareth, Jesus grew up with a sense of perspective and religious insight into the times. The body and mind grew in the expectation of many of the people.

Except for those who witnessed the birth of Jesus and were with him, the ordinary people who were not familiar with the existence of the boy Jesus were premature to accept Jesus as the Messiah, Jesus as the Son of God. As we read in the Bible, Jesus grew up with wisdom and intelligence as he grew up, and gradually had to stand through the days of childhood and boyhood to bear the work of the Messiah. This is to be regarded as the most precious period in his life, which assures the identity of Jesus as Son of God and Son of Man.

For Christ, born of the Son of God and the Son of man in the text, best understands the situation of millions of people who are in similar situations and whose growth processes are similar, and who have not hesitated to come down to their place of life because God had the most human appearance.

Jesus saves the people and frees them from the oppression of sin and the diseases. There is better understanding of the life of the people.

Jesus was one of them in those days. God who had the power to save the people sent his only son Jesus Christ. As God, Jesus Christ is therefore the greatest Savior of the people who suffer under sin, and become the Messiah.

The people suffer in all kinds of oppression and the bridges of life. When they look into their lives, they are caught up in miserable, evil spirits, and they can not save themselves. To save them, one must best understand them. He is Jesus Christ. The power to overcome sin is in God. The people themselves can never break the chain of sin. Because Jesus Christ is God, he can best understand the lives of the people and save them as God. That is why this book was written. In the Gospels we should note who Jesus met, what kind of conversation, and what he did.

COME DOWN INTO THE PEOPLE'S LIVES.

During the three years of public ministry, Jesus met mainly with people. Among the people he met, there were some who were high and learned, but most of them were the lost sheep of Israel. The lost sheep were people who did not seek anyone and were not interested in the mainstream society.

The people of the marginalized classes such as the tax collectors, the prostitutes, and the surrounding people who could not stand in the center of society, while being treated as sinners by the society were at there. Sometimes, when he spoke unflinchingly of his vested interests, he became a close friend to those who wander like a sheep without their keeper. He showed a good leader as a good shepherd who would guide them if they showed the right way to those who walked the wrong way.

Jesus stood on the side of the weak people of that day, thinking, advocating, and proclaiming the Word of God. Today, the church must stand on the side of the weak people and meet as many people as he did. Just as Jesus, not only in the church, but down to the scene of their lives and met them personally, Christians must come to the scene of their lives and stand, think, comfort and share the Word of God with the people.

If we refuse to meet with the neglected people and the Church is to be treated rather than entertained in association with the vested interests, only the empty beliefs that can not exercise any influence over the one religious zeal like the scathing scribes or religious leaders are echoed just like bells. The church is a holy place to be transformed from unclean to clean.

What was the role of the church so far? We should emphasize only the distinction of secularity and reflect on ourselves by asking whether we have not ignored the pain of them and ignored the church's original obligation and only devoted to quantitative growth.

From now on, it is time for the church to restore its role and function as the subject of change that transforms the world while preserving its identity as a church. In order to restore the purpose of the church's existence, the church should go into the field of people's life, breathe together, share their problems and communicate. As if Jesus had met and communicated with thousands of people in the field of miracles.

CHAPTER 1

HEALING PETER'S MOTHER IN LAW

Matthew 8: 14-15

"He touched her hand and the fever left her, and she got up and began to wait on him (Matthew 8:15)."

PETER HAD the most common person who could be found in there. He was an ordinary fisherman, the middle class in his day. He hired a worker, fishing together and holding several boats. The Bible does not make it clear who Peter's wife is. He only mentions his mother-in-law for a moment. Jesus was interested in this Peter's life. Peter, who is a fisherman and not so needy and has the most Jewish appearance, is attracted to and approached by the most civilized figure of the people, the innocent. There was the Lord's plan for Peter. The plan is the future ministry of the church through Peter and the work of the gospel.

Jesus calls the people and makes them disciples. And he gives them the work of God. This process, of course, involves the process of calling and training people. As a commoner, Peter, a man of the people, visited Peter's house and healed his mother-in-law. Peter was the most trustworthy person to trust in everything.

DOING MIRACLES OF THE PEOPLE

Jesus Christ was born as a son of man and grew up with people. The people he met were mainly those in the marginalized class who could be called the people of that age. He, the Son of God and the Son of Man, dwelt among the people and performed many miracles and powers. Jesus was a sufficient man.

There was always a clear purpose, and it was rather a joy to be with people. Why did he go through the Galilee, all Judea and Samaria, and perform the miracles and powers in the four Gospels? Through witnesses, he is testifying that he is the Messiah. Through the sign, he was to testify that he is the Messiah. They would not have followed Him as the Messiah if he had not done any miracles and power. They would have thought of Jesus as a rabbi or a sage who had nothing to do with them. However, Jesus did not hesitate at all to do the power and always wanted to welcome people that he had come as the Son of God by showing the power of God to people.

TO BE WITH THE PEOPLE IN THE LOW PLACE

He came to witness the word of God to proclaim the gospel to the people who were in the lowest places of the day. People will see and believe. Religion depends on something and history must be raised in front of the eyes. It is the people who want to follow what is visible.

Jesus did not refuse it. Instead, through ministry he wanted people to be receptive to what he said and to be interested in the kingdom of God. So Jesus did miracles and power to testify the gospel. He wants to let people know that they are the object to be loved. The people are marginalized. They are objects to be loved. Jesus did not turn away from their demands and wanted to show them his mercy and love. It is God's consideration for the man suffering from all sorts of diseases and demons. People are equal. Jesus did the same thing. It shows that it is God's love for a man who does not discriminate.

THE GOSPELS CONTAIN LIMITED TRANSCRIPTS.

The reporter of the Gospel wrote a miraculous article in the Gospel, although Jesus did many ministries and miracles.

There were also a few duplications in other Gospels. Why? That is to record the necessary miraculous signs many times in detail to testify that the Lord has come as a sure Messiah through the contents of the continuing ministry. All of the witnesses in the Four Gospels are 34 kinds. In this book, we will look at all these ministries in chronological order, and we will look at what Jesus, the Messiah, and needs through the miracles he showed in the lives of the people.

HEALING HIS MOTHER IN LAW

Jesus was always diligent. He was with his disciples, and he spent time in a community life and went out to the synagogue. The reason he went to the synagogue was to tell people the truth.

He spent most of his time teaching and witnessing the Word of God. Jesus had the appearance of a true educator of his day. He also enlightened people, awakened the ages, and healed the seriousness of sin, especially to look after them. He was always prepared and always led those who came to Him well by word. Because he was full of the Word, people always enjoyed gathering around Him. He did not just minister with a simple knowledge, but above all, he knew God deeply, and responded to people's requests with rich wisdom.

He first desires the word of God, and he also interpreted the Word a new way according to the law of the time. So many people had a spiritual depth to the extent that his teachings were more profound than any law and teaching they had ever heard and more accessible to people's minds. The fact that the Word is awake and full reveals much to Christians today. No matter how many times the era walks through the information age and the knowledge age, the depth of the word is not as deep. Spiritual depth is equally applicable to the times of Jesus and the times of today.

It was Peter's mother-in-law's first stop after Jesus got up and taught in the synagogue. Simon, Peter's mother-in-law, says she has a severe fever. Peter at that time did not know Jesus so deeply. He just knew Jesus as a rabbi.

This incident, which happened before the in-depth meeting with Jesus on Peter's boat, led Peter to become interested in Jesus and to be concerned with the law as usual, and Jesus' teaching came to him with a whole new teaching. Jesus does not pass through the lives of suffering people. As a person who knew everything, Peter was also a people, full of his thoughts, full of knowledge of the sea.

He recognized the spiritual world. He looked at Peter who was scarce and watched him for his future vision and hope. He has fixed it. He now tells him to live without hope any more and to live as strong and bold as he is with hope. Now Peter's condition has given up everything. He also gave up fishing and gave up everything for his Lord, including his own personal desires. He met the Lord and decided to live as a disciple, and he left his nets with his brothers and followed Him. His mother-in-law was caught in a fever and could not do anything. He decided to live as a disciple, but he came to the home with difficulty.

WHAT SHOULD YOU RELY ON WHEN YOU MEET DIFFICULTIES?

According to the Lord, everything seems to prosper, but it is not. Sometimes difficult things happen and suffer hardships they can not cope with. The important thing is that you have to overcome and win. It says not to be easy. Is this the reason that you decided not to give up and follow the Lord? If his(Peter) mother-in-law is sick, the son-in-law can not do anything and gives up being a disciple and returns to his past life, that's all.

The Lord knew Peter well. So, the first thing He wanted to do was solve Peter's family problems. He did not go to Peter's house alone. James and John also went with Him. The reason for bringing them was to make it clear through the miracle that their choices, which followed the Lord by doing miracles and showing them, were the right choice. Jesus rebuked the fever toward Simon's mother-in-law. The reason why He scolded the fever is not because mother-in-law was haunted. Jesus often rebuked the miracles. He saw a rough storm and rebuked it. He scolded it for the sickness.

This personified the disease. It means what he says as if he was speaking to it. He wanted to show the act of pushing out the fever vividly. Through the way of Jesus' ministry, we must understand the following points:

1)We must acknowledge the power and authority in Jesus' words.
Jesus did not get carried away by sickness. He was not taken to Satan. Jesus bound the sick under his power. So, by the power of God, all sicknesses are forced to kneel before Jesus.

Through this, we should also let our sickness kneel before our feet as Christians. You should not be dragged into a disease. Just as Jesus rebuked the fever, we should not be attracted to our body diseases.

As the Lord has done, you must overcome it by leading to the Lord's hand of power, King of kings. The Lord is with us when we want to overcome.

2)Jesus wanted to show that all things of nature are under the authority

of the Lord.
Jesus is the Creator God. As He is the Creator of all things, we must know that there is nothing to be impossible in his sight. Jesus stands on the side of the people. People are weak. They are those who need help. The Lord is willing to be with them. His ability to help the people, who are with the people, is incomparably greater than anything in the world. As soon as Jesus rebuked Peter's mother-in-law, the illness immediately went away. This is the holy authority of the Lord.

[Meditation point]

1) Why did Jesus come to this land and witnessed the miracle?
2) Why did the Lord come to preach the gospel of the kingdom and do miracles? Even today, the Lord is with us. To those who receive the gospel or the area where the gospel first enters, even today, the Lord does the power. He heals the sick, drives out demons, and many ministries of power appear to the saints in the church. The power and miracle work that the Lord had done 2000 years ago is still continuing. Why? For those who do not believe, it is an opportunity for repentance, and for those who believe, it is a victorious faith. It is for the sake of faithful faith in the Lord. The people are those who experience miracles. This can be said to be God's providence and work to accept the gospel.
3) At the beginning of the first ministry, He fixes Peter's mother-in-law. Let's think about the content and meaning of the text.
4) Have you ever thought of following or disobeying the Lord as a loss to me? Let's look at Peter. He gave up everything for the Lord. He lived hard for the Lord and his mother-in-law was ill. Jesus knew this Peter's heart and went into his house and healed his mother-in-law and comforted him.

"Lord, do not forsake me; be not far from me, O my God, Come quickly to help me, O LORD, my savior" (Psalm 38: 21,22).

5) Is there a disease in me? Do not you get carried away by the disease? Was not your heart fragile? He who is by my side is the one who loves me and is with me. The Lord was not drawn to sickness. He

conquered. He scolded it. We should not let the truth of our faith cool down because of the limits of my physical body.

"The LORD will sustain him in his sickbed,
and restore him from his bed of illness." (Psalm 41: 3)

CHAPTER 2

LORD WHO KNOWS MY WEAKNESS

Matthew 8: 16-17

"That evening came, many who were demon-possessed were brought to him, and he drove out the spirits with a word and healed all the sick. This was to fulfill what was spoken through the prophet Isaiah: 'He took up our infirmities and carried our diseases (Matthew 8:16-17)."

THE PEOPLE are weak. We are one of the people, who have no power, no property, no social background, and no strong supporters. They are weak but become strongest when they are together. The united people, the people who have gathered together, have hitherto been the most reforming and revolutionary ministry of human history.

Jesus' role is to establish a weak people. To this end, the Lord has dealt with all weaknesses. Wherever Jesus went, many weak people there came to Him. They were weakened by disease, and were gripped by the wicked spirit. The church should take care of the socially weak. It is the church's task to make them stand strong, not to condemn or criticize their weaknesses, but to overcome their weaknesses.

KNOWING THE TRUTH

One day the Rabbi of Israel spoke these words.
"The truth is like a stone on the road. The stone is a common thing to see here and there." His disciple asks the rabbi: "If truth is as common as a stone, why do not people know the truth easily?"

The rabbi gives this answer to the question of his disciples. "You have to bend your back to get a stone. Likewise, to get the truth, you must bend your back." We can not get the truth because we do not bow down. Through the words of the rabbi, we once again think about our attitude to know the truth. To know the truth, you have to bend your back. It should be lowered. When you have a humble heart and attitude, it means that truth can be mine.

God's Word is absolute truth. It is more truth than anything in the world. Then, in order to realize the Word of Truth and to know it, we must first be lowered and the proud waist bent. The world is in chaos and people lose their truth and wander. There is truth to save the world. To do that, we must know the teachings of Jesus. Why did he come to this earth? It is for the truth to free man. The freedom of truth brings us out of the snare of Satan. Everyone who hears the truth has a new life of survival. Through the work of miracles, people experience the true peace of truth. Jesus did the power and at the same time he taught what the truth was. The truth of Jesus who saved the world was the gospel.

There are so many countries in the world that countries need help. We must give them bread and the Gospel. That is the heart of Jesus. It is the mind of Jesus who wants to stand on the side of the weak. The only way to save the kingdom of the world is the word of the gospel and truth. Jesus came to this earth to find the weak. To those who reject the truth, who are arrogant and do not know how to bend their back, they will not accept it, no matter how much they testify of the gospel of life and the truth that sets it free. There are many words to be proclaimed, but few accept and receive them. So the way of truth is the way of life, and it is a narrow way. Through the text, we can discover the purpose that the Lord has come to this earth.

HE BRINGS MANY WEAK PEOPLE.

It was rumored that they brought the weaker socially. Jesus heals Peter's mother-in-law who loves Him. This is because he made Peter's decision worthy of all that he had left for the Lord and devoted himself to pursue the truth. Jesus healed the mother-in-law's disease so that it would not harm his followers. These rumors spread to all the towns, so who is Jesus? It brought those who have suffered from various diseases to the Lord.

A righteous ministry, good work should be rumored. The contents of the rumor are true and false. False rumors are inflated rumors. It creates an unfounded rumor and exaggerates it. These rumors are rumors of killing people. It is a rumor not to spread. When a person skips a person, the word will be different. Eve, who has eaten the fruit, is different because she eats the forbidden fruit. God told them not to eat, but they exchanged words as if they could be eaten. It was an excuse for Adam to eat fruits with the invitation of Eve and to come out of their mouths. Hiding behind the bushes in the Word of God, they commit sin to one another. They assume responsibility.

For the first time in humanity, false rumors have spread. This is the result of sin. The iniquity of mankind comes from hearing. When he hears Satan's words, he hears Eve's words and becomes guilty. These rumors are rumors that lead to death. But there are rumors to save people. It is the faith that comes from listening. The rumor from the text was a rumor of faith from the hearing. The good news of Jesus, who made clear about Jesus' healing of his mother-in-law and about the purpose of coming to this land, spread to all the towns, and people came to Him. The true people are those who put their weaknesses before the Lord.

"That evening, people brought many people who were demonized and suffered. Jesus saved those who suffered in their hearts, and He healed those who were sick. Jesus accomplished Isaiah's famous sermon. He suffered our pain, and weighed our diseases. (Eugene Peterson, Message / Matthew 8: 16, 17)"

People brought demon-possessed persons. You can tell how big the power of the demon is when you say that you have brought it a lot. The demon is a spiritual being. It is the evil spirit that Satan beats. If you are caught by the power of demons, you become a servant to Satan. You will be dragged around. Those who are caught in the forces of demons can be said to be suffering in their hearts.

The meaning of suffering in the mind is that people who are caught in the power of the demon feel common. If you hear an evil spirit, you have no peace in your heart, and you are always anxious. It is not what you think. In it, the forces of demons do not let the man catch him and freely. It is always anxious, and even difficult to control your actions. Jesus is the best counselor, the best man. Many of the demon-possessed people, the people who suffered in their hearts because of sin, came out and cast out demons without one being excluded. To win the power of demons means to have a stronger spirit than an evil spirit. The Spirit is the Spirit of the power of Christ. It is only the power of Jesus.

In the Word, Jesus says He has driven out all the forces of demons. And in the text, He says that he has cast out demons with the Word. The way to confront the evil spirit is the word of truth, which means that the word is important.

Anyone who knows the Word and believes in the power of the Word can resist Satan by His Word. Here is why we should study the Word. Even Jesus said that He not only cast out devils with the Word, but healed the disease with the Word.

Why did Jesus chase the gospel, heal the heart, and heal the sickness? This is to testify that the Messiah promised in the Old Testament was Jesus. Isaiah clearly speaks of Jesus' ministry. It is He who is responsible for our own weakness and who has carried our illnesses. It is. To say that we are weak is to know our weaknesses. The Lord knows better than anyone that I am weak.

He wanted to let you know through the Word that you are trying to understand more than anyone else our stumbling, hardship, and difficulty. People try to pretend to be strong. When we see people these days, we pack ourselves well. We like to show off our ability. So nowadays there is a lot of pride in the world. If you listen, you are self-proud. It boasts money, boasts of appearance, power, boasts of home, and so on.

Boasting is not a bad thing in itself. Behind the heart that wants to brag, all of you can wrap yourself in pretty wrapping paper and feel that you want to give it to people. We are ashamed to let go of what is not. In that state, no ability appears. You will have to unpack the wrapper to find out what the contents are inside. Packaged gifts must be removed. There is no object in the world to use without breaking. Likewise, God wants to use me. Then God removes all the things that are wrapped around me. What does God want? It is painful to bring the weaknesses into the Lord unpacked. Why? This is because our Lord came to this land because of my weakness. For we have come to earth to bear our weaknesses on the shoulders of the Lord to carry them directly.

{Meditation Point}

1)Why did people bring many sick people, to Jesus? Do I have a good sense of distinction between good rumors and bad rumors? How much did I hear and testify for faith?
2)Who are they who came to Jesus, and how did he heal them? What is my weakness? It is all my disease that I have hurt in my life. We must know that the Lord wants us to take over.

CHAPTER 3

CHANGING IN CHRIST

John 2: 5-11

"And the master of the banquet tasted the water that had been turned into wine. He did not realize where it had come from, though the servants who had drawn the water knew. Then he called the bridegroom aside (John 2:9)."

THROUGH MANY generations, it has always undergone a period of change. Newly started history always opens with change. If it does not change, it will not be renewed. The Bible says, "Be transformed by the renewing of your mind (Romans 12:2)." It is a fundamental ethical practice that Christians must accept. It begins with the imitation of Christ first. Christ is the standard for all forms of life. The life of Christ determines Christians' life.

Therefore, anyone who wants to be a Christian must be modeled after Christ's life. We must give all our beings in righteousness and obedience, based on his mind, actions, and all things. Do not follow the vain things of the world. Such things do not help change because change is a whole new thing. The things of the world are all gone, but there is nothing new under the sun. There is no real change expected. Change does not start from the head. Change is experiencing life in itself. And I live by following the Lord's guidance and emotion. The mind, soul and body of man are connected. There is a saying, Chinese characters, "以(Yee)心(Sim)傳(Chun)心(Sim): We share moments of warmth and emotion from heart to heart." The trees are connected by roots and share nutrients together.

If I first get caught up in the inner emotions of the Holy Spirit, I will share and feel what I feel and receive along with my conscience along with my heart. I can not change others unless I change first.
Who are the weak? They are desperate for change and those who want to share and feel together. In the times, the people demanded change and threw themselves into the scene of history. And they experienced change, and sometimes they did not. The Lord transforms water into

wine and adds to the excitement of the feast. It brings true joy to people. The Lord is the subject of change. And every one is sharing the joy of change together. To who does change happen? It is the hearts of the people. But the mind is not the only one who can do everything by itself. It is a heart that falls to the power of Christ. Humility is the best virtue that the people have. If you lay yourself down before Christ for longing for change, the Lord will fill their hearts with rich spiritual joy.

LET'S TURN WATER INTO WINE.

In the text, a miracle occurs in which water turns into wine. Wine is liquid, and water is liquid. However, the liquid is the same in nature, but the ingredients are completely different.

This is what it means to be a Christian. I can say that I am changed in Christ. We who believe in Christ must be entirely new, as children of perfect God. A sinner is called righteous by faith. I have no past. It is the new I am now transformed by the Lord. Then what if we want to change in Jesus Christ? Here is the secret of change.

YOU MUST BE INVITED TO THE FEAST.

The water turned into wine. People enjoy the delight of the feast while enjoying the delicious wine. Here, let's assume that you were not invited to a feast. You can not taste delicious wine. And I will not even hang out with people. When the guests were invited to the feast, they did not go anywhere else.

I did not even leave during the feast. All those who kept to the end enjoyed the taste of the wine with the water changed. Jesus invites us to the feast of heaven. Then, as an invited person, you should not reject it. When the feast of the gospel and the feast of life are opened, they must go to the feast house. And we must be with the Lord until the end. The people are invited as guests to a banquet house.

They have the right to legitimately possess joy and the right to experience miracles in the field of change. You will be able to join in the field of the Lord's abilities when you are patient and remain in the invited feast. You should not miss churches with excuses to be busy.

The scene of worship is a holy time to meet the Lord.

The more I reject worship, the more I refuse to hear the gospel, and the more I reject it, the more I will be separated from the grace of God. Christians must keep their place. You should not break the joy of the feast. We should listen to the gospel and rejoice together and know the grace of God. Then the joy is full. This joy is not temporary but must be continued even after the feast is over. To do that, we must be close to the Lord. You should not leave the scene.

The apostle John testified that everyone who receives Him, who believes in his name, has given himself the authority to become a child of God (John 1:12).

The people are weak and innocent. They can not refuse the place where they have been called. They first enter into grace by being with the Lord. Whatever you do, wherever you go, you must be an invitee, just like the second verse. If you invite the Lord, you will be willing to go with us. And there will be miracles.

YOU NEED TO KNOW WHAT THE PROBLEM IS.

You need to know what's wrong. Mary was the first to discover the problem of falling wine. Mary believed in Jesus and ran to the invited Jesus to talk about the problem. If wine falls out of common sense, to whom should I go? That is the owner of the house. But Mary did not go to her master and went to Jesus. What does it mean? He knew that only the Lord could solve the problem. Everywhere is always a problem. It is important to ask who you are when the problem arises. In the first chapter of 2Kings, Ahaziah is ill. The illness was injured. But because of the wound he can not come down from the bed.

Ahaziah does not ask God about his illness, but goes to Baal-Zebub and asks. God tells him this. "Do you go to the idol and ask, because there is no God in Israel? You will not leave the bed you are lying on, you will certainly die." Ahaziah, who does not ask God, is ultimately complicated by trauma, and can not come down from the bed and finish his life. When you have a problem, it is important to depend on who you are.

Mary is also a human being and a frail person who must pray to Jesus. It was the prayer title that she had no wine. It is important that we pray specifically when we pray. What is my prayer subject? We must give that prayer. In Mary's saying, He writes extreme and says, "What does a woman have to do with me? My time has not come." Jesus showed that Mary's request was accepted and that it would be done when the time had come. It will be when the time comes. When you have a problem, you need to pray. Praying to the Lord should be habitual. The Lord said that only those who have learned to pray can pray. And when you start praying, you say that it is the beginning of miracles. All changes come from prayer.

THE SECRET OF CHANGE IS OBEDIENCE.

Jesus said to the servants, "Fill the jar with water." What they need is not grape juice. They could deny or dispute an unreasonable order. But it was not. The stone jar was a huge sheep that could be drunk for about 300 people, even though ten rounds were returned to one person.

The sheer volume of water turned into wine. It turned out to be the best in quantity and quality. People did not know why, but the servants knew who was asking them to take the water in the jar and why the miracle of such change took place. Mary and servants were closest to the miracle scene.

They thoroughly believed and obeyed the Lord. Mary told them to do as he pleased. And the servant was the one who actually received the water in the field, but they were obedient. The miraculous real change in the field of faith does not lie within the framework of rational reason. In other words, it is not understood only by the head and realized. A person of miracles, everyone in faith, is a person who has experienced power in irrational and irrational matters. The work of all miracles of the Bible took place in such an environment.

ABILITY TO BE CONNECTED EACH OTHER

They became one with obedience. They became one to one, brought water to the stone jar, filled it, and filled it. No one rejected or disobeyed. A miracle happened when one mind became one. They show the people without power. They were oppressed by their masters and were forced to live as servants. When they saw it personally, there was no power and weakness, but when they were united and brought water with one mind, miraculous work arose. The people are weak in personal view, but they exert great power when they form a unity and a community of people.

THE SECRET OF CHANGE WAS THE GLORY OF THE LORD.

In verse 11, he performed his first sign in Cana and showed his glory, saying that his disciples believed in Jesus. The word glory is a holy term used exclusively by God in the Bible. However, through the wine incident, he showed the glory of Jesus.

What does this mean? It means that the glory of the holy and omniscient God appeared through Jesus. It is God who will be glorified through miraculous ministry. Jesus came to show the glory of God and because of the miracles that Jesus has made, people will glorify Him and believe Him as God. So the disciples came to believe that Jesus was sent by God.

Jesus is the life. Jesus, who raises and transforms people, is the object of faith that we must trust and depend on. We must live in this faith. What is Jesus in your faith? Is it merely meeting our needs? Are you just looking for something when you need it? Jesus is the object of our faith. It is a hope for all. We must live with the hope of change. We have to change. We must see here that our future depends.

"Do not expect my surroundings to change, but I will first be changed and become a man of good faith, so that I can change my surroundings."

"True change starts from me."

"Be a man like wine that can give joy and good to others."

{Meditation Point}

1)Have you ever been invited to a feast? What was the joy of that time? Do I, having been invited to the feast, have joy with the Lord? Or I would like to look back on myself if the body is not in another place in the feast.

2)What about my experience of experiencing and coping with the

problem?
3)What should we do to obey the Word?

CHAPTER 4

GO! YOUR SON IS ALIVE.

John 4: 46-54

"Go," Jesus replied, "your son will live." The man took Jesus at his word and departed (John 4:50)."

IN GENESIS, Jacob is exhausted from his brother's pursuit, sleeping on a stone pillow at the place called Bethel. It was the most powerful days of Jacob. When no one is near Jacob, God shows his vision to Jacob in dreams. The fantasy was the ladder connected to the sky, and the angels ascending and descending the ladder.

For Jacob, it was the first time in his dream that he had the comfort and conviction of God. Before that, he received faith education through his mother Rebekah. How God has worked in the family of Isaac. God, who only heard with his ears, came to see through dreams.

It was the mother Rebecca's decision to go to Laban's house. He began by listening only to his mother's advice, but through this dream, Jacob shifts his viewpoint from man to God. The ladder with which the earth and the sky are connected is God's message to tell Jacob that there is still hope in despair that should not be forsaken.

Faith has the power to get hope in despair. Even if you give up everything, if you have faith, let it rise again. Today, many Christians underestimate the power of faith. We think of the history of faith as if it were a story in the Bible. Who are the people? They are those who live right away and experience the history of faith. They are people who need faith. In order to live as a true Christian, we must have faith to confess and experience the fact that God has not forsaken and has been with Him.

THERE IS A STAGE OF DEVELOPMENT IN FAITH.

In the text, a person who has nothing to do with faith comes up with a story that overcomes his crisis. The Bible says that he is the king's servant. Perhaps it was one of the servants of Herod Antibas. At that time, the king's servant was a person who had considerable power, wealth, and influence on the society.

However, his son suffered a serious disease. Every effort was made to restore a son, but all his efforts were in vain. More and more death moments were approaching. At this time he heard rumors about Jesus. He heard it was a miracle man made of water with wine. For them, Jesus was the last wish to live. He had no choice but to go to Jesus. The text tells us what happened to his servant and how his faith grows.

THE STEPS OF THE DEVELOPMENT OF THE FAITH OF THE KING'S SERVENT

1)It is a faith that hangs on miracles.

The son's father hung on a miracle. He had no faith. There was only one thought. It only miraculously happened to a son who did not heal by means of all human healing. We are relieved of the faith of the Father. It is like a child looking at miracles. You should not think of it as. Children like miracles. They are imaginative. We must live in imagination. His father was the same. The father had only one idea that he wanted his son to live no matter what. If anyone could save his son, it was his desire to live. He says, "Let my son live." Jesus answers his petition. "Without a miracle, you do not believe." He was saddened when he saw people hanging only in signs and miracles. However, Jesus did miracles and preached the Word.

Why did he do that? It is because the petition of those who want miracles is not wrong. It is natural for anyone to wish for a miracle to someone who has been in trouble. But the problem is that you have to realize that this stage is a very immature place of faith. Belief in miracles can be accepted as the beginning of the first faith. At first we begin to believe in Jesus through small miracles around us. People around him are healed, demons leave, and the problems of life are resolved like miracles. And the thought of the Lord alive comes to the world of faith. This step is a step in between us. Are you in crisis? Need help? Was the wish to live cut off? You must come to Jesus. And we must believe in the power of the Lord. We must pray for miracles. You should start there. But you should not stay at this stage. You have to move on to the next step.

2) *It is a stage of faith that accepts and believes the Word.*

The servant did not know the intention of Jesus. And he asks again. "Please come before I die." But did Jesus' response go right to his servant? It is not. He just proclaimed the Word in verse 50. "Go! Your son lived." The servant came to Jesus personally to lay hands on him and pray that he would pray. But it was not.

Jesus wanted his faith to mature a little. He wanted a faith that relied solely on the Word, believing, and returning, rather than a miracle that would soon be visible. But an amazing thing happened. The servant believed the word of Jesus and said he went. The servant has now passed from a faith that requires miracles to a stage of faith that holds the Word. The fact that the servant just returned from believing the Word was just like a miracle. This tells us that the foundations of the faith of the servant have changed. He no longer relied on himself. He did not count on his own wishes.

It was the words of Jesus that he began looking and relying on. It began to be based on that word. If the foundation of our faith is not based on Jesus' words, but on us, our faith will shake according to circumstances. The foundation of our faith must be the Lord, not I. The Lord says, "My words will not go away." The foundation of faith is not the expectation or hope in my heart; it must be the word of God. Pastor Torrey said to the Bible students, what is it that you are living in faith every day? He said I am a believer in the Word of God. The students replied, Hold on to the Word and live. And the pastor says, you do not hold the Word, but the Word must hold you. In the midst of crisis, in the midst of trouble, you have to hold on to the Word, and the Word must hold you up.

3) *It is the faith that saves the family.*

The faith of the servant saved not only himself but his son, and the whole family. In verse 53, "The father knew that it was the time when Jesus said that he had lived, and he and all his people believed." The good things Jesus did are revealed. Darkness can not hide the light. Things like the servant's testimony and miracles were communicated to the family, and they were saved. Jesus did not go to the place where the Son lay, but healed it with the Word only. The place where Jesus was is Cana, and the house of the servant was in the north. On the streets, it was fixed only by the Word, which was several tens of kilometers away.

At the same time, the son was alive. He did not live as soon as he arrived, but lived as soon as he spoke. The servant would have thought about the time he went back and healed. When the owner asked time, the servants reported that it was 7 pm (about 1 pm in modern time). According to verse 53, that was when Jesus declared, "Your son lived." And by word of mouth, it was the salvation of all the family. "Your son is alive." This word was a word that gave hope to the family as well as the servant. This is comforting. Today, the Lord gives us the same word. "We have solved your problem." As soon as the problem is solved, Jesus gives more grace and blessing. Just as Jesus gave his servant the healing of the son and the salvation of his family, Jesus also gives us a greater gift when we come to faith. We, humans, live in time, space, or constraints. But Jesus transcends time and space. The Holy Spirit is always with me wherever I am. My body is here now, but when I pray for my family here, the Lord is there. When I intercede, the Lord is on the scene of the prayer. Even though our bodies are separated from each other, we are able to experience the power of our prayers and the power of faith because the Lord is always with us.

I heard a deacon bear a testimony that this deacon was always a prayerful person, and one day the prayers of his brethren who lived far away were eagerly awaited. So, he prayed that day and then he came back home after praying. He got a call from his brother in the evening, and he was in a hospital because he was in a traffic accident trying to cross the street that day. He was not hurt so much and he's fine. He asked the time of the accident and it was the very time that he was praying in the church. They all praised God's grace, prayer, and faith in God's work. Does this story only apply to the deacon? It is the story of those who ask by all faith.

[Meditation]

1)What stages is our change of faith? Do I believe and rely on the Word? Or is it still in the position of looking at miracles?

CHAPTER 5

GET UP, TAKE YOUR PLACE AND WALK!

John 5: 1-15

"But he replied, the man who healed me told me, pick up your mat and walk (John 5:11)."

JESUS' LIFE was a life with the weak people.
He went into their place of life, laughed together, cried together, healed their pain, and sometimes led the people who walked the wrong way with a strict teacher.

The life of Jesus, who is also a close friend of the people, is the direction of the ministry to which the church should be directed today. What is a church? The church is a place of healing. It is the place where the word of God is proclaimed and the healing takes place by the Word. Who should be treated and what? It is a people. People are persons who need help. They can not stand up themselves.

The people are not proud. Their hearts are not high. They are poor, meek, and clean. They are always hungry for truth and interested in it. The church should go to the job of helping them to get into their lives and stand together. The church is the lower place where the people come. The spectacular appearance of the church never attracts public attention. The pastor's brilliant career and rhetoric, and the well-organized program of the church, are not the good attractions. Those who have a good conscience, such as Jesus Christ, and who have a shepherd's heart, should visit the people's lives. There is a church in which God is pleased to begin.

LET'S GO INTO THE LIFE OF THE PEOPLE.

It was a Jewish holiday. The feast of the text was probably Pentecost. Jesus was a keeper of the feast. At that time, there was an obligation to go to Jerusalem and worship in the temple in the national holidays. Because of his duty, Jesus also came to Jerusalem. But something that can not be understood will happen. Of course, we must go to the temple and worship, but Jesus did not go to the temple but went to the wrong place. It is a place called Bethesda Pond. We have to think about why he went to the pond there. Feast is a season to enjoy with people. But Jesus came to those who were not able to get along with the people and was suffering from their problems.

JESUS'S CONCERN WAS WITH THE SICK.

Jesus' concern was with sick people. Jesus came to those who had physical and spiritual ills. The Bethesda pond, not the temple, was a place full of all kinds of intruders. It was the place where the sick people suffering from illness, all kinds of people who did not have anything, and sinners gathered. The reason they were there was to get better. Healing was only waiting for the water to move around the pond, because only the first person to enter the water moved, and only one was getting healing. They had no idea of a holiday. They could not imagine going to the temple to worship.

There was only one way to get better. Once the water moved, great confusions came up. Even if they tread on each other and hit each other, only those who were strong could get better. It was a miniature of a competitive society. It could not find the holy temple of Jerusalem. Today, our society is similar to this. The world is a competitive society. It fights struggling to win the competition. If you can only succeed, there is no matter whether you die or live. Someone used the term 'cruelty' to refer to the society in which we live. A ruthless society, an unrecognized society, a material misconception that everything is in the hands of a material makes the world that people live harder. Bethesda in 2000years ago, and this world we live in was not much different from Bethesda.

The world is full of sick people as sinners. They are just looking at each other's opportunities. Jesus should know why he did not go to the holy temple but to Bethesda. The Lord has entered the world. He moved his feet to Bethesda to heal the sick and sinners there.

JESUS WANTED TO SHOW WHAT GOD IS LIKE.

He wanted to show that Jesus is the God of love. The temple in which God is present had the Most Holy Place but did not go. Who was there in Jerusalem?
There were Pharisees, scribes, and institutions that persecuted Jesus, who were obsessed with religious authority. It was not a place worthy of love. Religious leaders had no love. They thought that they were clean without sin. Their heart was high and arrogant.

God's love can not come to such people. Rather, those who should be loved were not in the temple but in the pond. He had to go to the place where the people who were oppressed were gathered and to convey the love of God. He went to the Bethesda Pond where the suffering people were there to witness the love of God. In the pond there were losers who were completely defeated in the competitive society. There is no power. It was a place full of despair. There Jesus wanted to be a hope.

LET'S MEET THE SUFFERING PEOPLE.

Jesus looks around the pond. And he points to the one who is the most unjust and barren. He had been completely destroyed by disease for 38 years.

The religious leaders also referred to him as a cursed person. He could not move his body, he just lie down and envied others who be cured. He could not do anything.

It was such a pitiful life that he lived in the world because he could not die like the trash that was abandoned. Jesus asks the poor man. He did not treat it from the beginning. First, he asked if there is a will in the mind to heal.

"Do you want to be better?" This is a question everyone knows. Jesus asked that the willingness to be well is important. Without a will, miracles do not happen. For 38years, he was willing to plant himself once again in the race, where he has not been motivated to go out of the competition. Those who wake up today are those whose will is still alive.
The sick answer in verse 7. "I want to get better, but nobody can put

me in the pond." He said. It is where love has cooled down. We could not find any unity without reconciliation. It was a target for everyone to step on the competition. These places are desperate. Jesus told him three words. 'Get up!' 'Take your seat!' and 'Walk!'

1)Get up! He said. The word 'wake up' means to wake up but not to lay down. Only a person can stand upright. The word to get up is to see the heaven. It means to look at the living God, not just the things on the earth. If you do not get up, you can not walk. You always have to sit down with a sense of defeat.

2)Take the seat! Jesus makes a greater demand. Just sit back and relax. It was his position that sustained him for 38years. The only will was the seat. For him, the bed was like all his being. He could not live without relying on it for a day. But get up and take the place. This is no longer the place for his master. Now the master has taken his seat and proclaimed himself as the line. When he was lying down, the seat controlled the entire person. But the place that got up and held in his hand is now able to move at will. You can take your seat and throw it away. He was a miracle to live an independent life.

3)Walk! For 38years he was unable to walk one step, and he was asked to step forward for the first time. Go forward. It means not to sit still and despair, but to go forward. To walk means to give a new mission to the person. The past life has been cleaned and now it has become a new person to live a new life for the glory of God.

For 38years he was tamed in illness. It is a habit. He was helplessly exposed to the disease. He could not do anything. Whatever this habituation is scary. Once you get tired of habits, it's hard to get out of there. It is hard to stand up once the habit of sin has fallen once in a while and it has fallen continuously and has now become a habit. Jesus does not want it. Above all, I want to stand up and claim my life and move forward. God wants me to be the master of my life, but he wants me to live a dignified life while pioneering our destiny. To do so, we must also listen to the Lord's voice.

LET'S EXPRESS US.

Jesus pointed to himself and said that he worked hard. He said that because God works, he also works. Jesus healed the sickness for 38 years on the Sabbath day. What is the Sabbath day? It is a day to worship and serve God. Jesus healed a man on the Sabbath day, the day of worship of God. Because of this, many were persecuted because of the Jews' time and temptation, but Jesus always enjoyed doing God's work. We must work as Jesus did. We do not know how many the 38 years sick are around us. There are many people who do not believe in Jesus and are desperate. We must work diligently. Go to them and testify of the gospel and help them to rise again.

'Get up!' 'Take your seat!' 'Walk!' These three words mean that you have to lay back and work again, but not longer. And if you have one more word, then verse 14, "Do not sin again!" A worker, a man enthralled by a holy passion, has no place to sin. I do not give a chance to sin because I am working. This means to be a Saints who are always awake by their work.

{Meditation Point}

1)Let's turn around. And let's think about it. This place we live in is like a Bethesda pond. How do I look there?
2)What is in me like a habit, what makes me helpless and captivated by defeat?

CHAPTER 6

NOW GO OUT WHERE IT IS DEEPER.

Luke 5: 1-11

"When he had finished speaking, he said to Simon, Now go out where it is deeper, and let down your nets to catch some fish (Luke 5:4)."

PEOPLE ARE pure and they are like a child. If Jesus does not lead them to the side, they are like those who have lost their way. The people of this age need a good teacher. It is not the wrong way to go to the right side, but the way of life if you go this way, not the wide way of destruction. You need a leader who teaches and guides you that you can live together even if you are tough.

People without leaders are those who have lost the meaning of true freedom. A country or organization that does not have one awakened leader reaches indulgence. No one can control it, power is abused, and the economy is down. In it, the people must live in pain that can not be said. The absence of a leader entices the people into their lives. They do not want to listen to anyone. They know that their own is the best. They reject the truth. Leaders are those who awaken such people, and give new mission.

Life is like the sea. And people are looking at only the fish that they will not be caught in any trouble, but still throwing a wasteful net into the sea. The people who do not have a leader will be in vain no matter how hard they try. All that is raised is an empty net. There is only a waste of the net in the sea of life. Leaders awaken those who live in vain life, and return them to the sea of truth.

We must listen to the voice of the truth that the people turn around and turn away the wrong way.

WHAT HAPPENED AT GENNESARET

In other words, Gennesaret is also called Sea of Galilee, Tiberias. It was originally a lake, but its width and depth were wide and deep and called sea. This is where the earth was fertile and cultivated a lot of crops, and there was a lot of seafood in the sea. People got a lot from the sea to live. The risk was followed, but the abundant life was guaranteed. Peter from the text was a fisherman. He had two ships with other business partners. Peter and his companion came out of two boats and were grooming the net.

The ship was empty. There was no fish in the net. In verse 1 people came to the shore and listened to the Lord. There was always a desire for the Word, so they chased him away without distinction wherever the Lord had gone. There were those who were willing to listen to the words, but there were people who gave up listening to them for their own work and were enthusiastic about their lives. The crowds were Peter and his associates.

On one side he listened to the word, on the other he was indifferent to the spiritual life, devoted to his life. Jesus came to the beach and saw them washing the net. And when he had risen up to twice as much as he had taught on the ship, he said to go deep into Peter. Suddenly he is finished with the message and goes deep. Jesus came to the boat and taught the Word, and Peter heard it.

Peter also listened to his life for a while. As the Word comes into it, it begins to pay attention to spirituality.

Jesus told Peter to go deep and go down into the net to catch the fish once. Now Peter's heart is exhausted. It is not easy to survive than thought. He has to keep a livelihood to catch fish, but now Peter had nothing to do with it. He tried to catch the fish all night but could not catch it. His feelings were in desperate condition. It was a position to return without any harvest. He tried to fix Peter's wrong thinking that he thought he (Peter) was a failure. So, deep down, he asked Peter to go down the net.

Jesus wanted Peter to enter the deep spiritual world. It meant that you could not do anything in your life until now, and in life without income, you should try to experience rich income by relying on the Lord once.

Peter, who listened to him until now, said, "Lord, I did not have any harvest even though I worked all night." Peter, a fisherman, is more specialized in catching fish.

But now Peter's suffering does not depend on his experience or his knowledge. He intends to depend on Jesus thoroughly. So, by relying on the words of Jesus, he was led by two ships to the deep sea.

EXPERIENCE WHAT YOU HAVE NEVER EXPERIENCED BEFORE.

When he took the Lord with his heart and went down into the depths and lowered the net, tremendous fish was caught. There are so many that the net is torn and the fish is caught enough to fill twice. It was a moment when all the failures and hurts of the past day were compensated to those who had just lost their nights. Jesus is the one who keeps his promises. When we relied on the net, a miracle work arose. The deep sea is full of all kinds of fish and treasures. Now we can see where the fish are coming from with the fish finder, but that was not the case.

We just went to a place where fish was and relied on our own experience to bring down the net. When Peter did so, nothing was raised. When you depend on yourself, nothing has happened. However, when he gave up on his own, he took much fish. We must rely on and obey the Lord's Word. If you ask the Lord to go deep, you must go. There is no room for the Lord's will. Our Lord is the one who does not make mistakes. It is not my experience or knowledge that leads me, but only one Lord Jesus.

A philosopher (Kierkegaard) distinguished three ways in which the people of the world live.

A person who thinks that he is the most important and must stand in the center(People who depend on themselves, who live by feeling their own emotions)

An ethical person who takes the rights of others more seriously than oneself(A person who lives ethically and morally, who does not harm others)

A person interested in the spiritual world

He is a spiritual person, a person who pursues spiritual things while considering the world of deep spirituality. The noblest life is a person who knows the spiritual world and lives by looking at it. Everybody knows the shallow seaside. Outside the water, the water is visible. Most people can not escape from this shallow beach level. We do not care if I talk about the deep sea. There is no interest in telling the secret of experiencing the history of miraculous history richness, even if the spiritual world is told. Peter went after the Lord's intention to go down into the depths and let down the nets, and after he took many fish, he became aware of the Lord's heart.

Peter's spiritual eyes have been opened.

It was the first time to set foot on the spiritual deep world. Anyone who knows Jesus deeply will experience this experience. Such a world that we have never known before is opened. When I enter the world, I know who I am. I know that I am a sinner. Peter looked back on his life so far. The past lived for one person. Just as the fish was caught that day, he was feeling better and he was disappointed and he was caught up in the amount of fish caught. There was no joy in the heart. However, after seeing the word of the Lord, the joy of the spirit that was unknown until now was overflowed. So he fell down before the Lord and confessed, "Lord, leave me, I am a sinner."

Many people were amazed when they saw the flesh in v. 9. James and John, who became Peter's partner and later became loyal disciples of Jesus, were amazed. They believed in their own strength and lived to this day, and as a result, they were the ones who had made nothing but gain their lives.

It was a recovery. Peter and his colleagues did not have a problem with caught fish. There was no heart in it. He has met Him who is most important in his life. In his life, he met a master he should serve. He is the one who fills two times. It is the abundant Lord who fills all our spiritual and physical lives.

Jesus said to Peter, "Do not be afraid. Now you will be a fisher of men." He led Peter into the life of a fisherman who was catching people. He has called Peter to be the apostle of the great God who will witness the gospel and establish the church all over the world. This event was a great event that changed Peter for a lifetime. If Peter had given up accepting the Lord at the time, there would be no one to know Peter today. But when Peter received the Lord, became a fisherman who realized himself, there was such a remarkable work that today a church was built on the confession of Peter, and Peter was recognized as the great apostle of the Lord.

Peter's life is not the life of failure. Peter met with Jesus and his life turned into the life of a great apostle who witnessed the gospel to all the people of the world in the life of the Galilee fishermen. A double-filled fish is a visual showing what Peter's ministry will be like in the future. He showed that the life of the followers of the Lord is like this.

We are the same. According to the Lord, our ship is not empty ship. It is the abundant ship that the Lord has always filled.

{Meditation Point}

1)Genesaret is a beach. Maybe our lives are a miniature of life. However, we live in this sea like a pouring of water under the vine, with no harvesting, only vain effort.
We can not find a meaningful life without experiencing a deep spiritual world. If we live spiritually, we must listen to the word of the Lord. How are we now?
2)How far do I approach the deep spiritual world? How much do I hear the call of the Lord? Is my ship empty now? Or is your mission filled with vision? Are you listening to the voice of the Lord?

CHAPTER 7

THE AUTHORITY OF WORD

Mark 1: 21-28

"Amazement gripped the audience, and they began to discuss what had happened, what sort of new teaching is this? They asked excitedly, it has such authority! Even evil spirits obey his orders (Mark 1:27)."

THE LANGUAGE we use also has a scent. The language tells all of the personality without hiding it. The language, the environment, the current situation, and the personality that have grown up are kept intact. The shepherd should raise the sheep in good language. Sheep hears the voice of the shepherd. There are indigenous people living in Almaty, Kazakhstan. If there is a precious guest there, it is said that the best food is cooking the sheep. However, he is said to give his children special areas first, the mouth and ear of sheep. The reason for giving good things to the children is that they want them to grow up.

As language has a scent, good language and sound warms the heart and brings happiness. But there are words to kill. It is a word that destroys the soul. It does not give life, hope and it is desperation. Where is the church? It is the place where the sound of killing souls is not proclaimed, but the voice of grace that saves lives. The Word of God has a remarkable ability to revive the dying soul. The people must survive through words. Through the word, the sleeping soul must wake up. Just as the Word of God's authority revives the man, the word of the Lord proclaimed in today's church must be the ability to save the people.

The word to study today is the ministry of Jesus' early activity. Relatively, Jesus was free to enter the synagogue. People who came to the synagogue often could think of Jesus as one of many rabbis. Jesus, who would have been regarded as one of the ordinary people, began to be seen in human eyes with a totally different perspective on the text. It was the authority of the Word that people have never encountered before. Jesus' teachings were without precedent. He called himself

Christ, set up the law again, and dealt with the leaders of the temple. And he collided with them. Jesus threw himself in a righteous way, but he wanted to correct the wrong thing.

JESUS' REACTION TO SURPRISE PEOPLE

In verse 22, people say that they were amazed at their teaching. He was astonished when he saw the power of healing a man caught in evil spirits and even letting evil spirits kneel before the authority of the Word. People even point to this as a new and powerful lesson. That teaching and action were a new dimension that they have never experienced before. The Gospel of Mark mentions this as spiritual authority. This authority, which only Jesus had, was even jealous and jealous of the Jewish leaders who had power before God and who did not have this authority on the other hand. There is nothing as innocent as a human heart. The Jewish leaders tried to bring down the man who had that authority (the authority that Jesus had) because they did not have it. They were jealous of envy and jealousy that they were not there. They were the ones who refused if they thought it would hurt them to the end.

AUTHORITY OF JESUS

A DIFFERENT AUTHORITY THAN THE SCRIBE

The authority of the teaching of Jesus was different from the scribes. Here we can see what the authority of Jesus is by examining what authority scholars have taught based on. The scribes are the ones who have mastered the best scholars of the time.
If it is the same nowadays, the house is also excellent in the best prestigious university. Their thoughts coincided with the politics and culture of the nation. Political power was demonstrated, too, and social position was high-class people. He studied the law from a young age, and worked for a lifelong copy of the Bible.

Because of their dedicated efforts, Judaism remained a national spirit in the colonial society. Other religions also had religious zeal which they could not follow. If this is the case, the authority should be different. They have to overwhelm people. However, it did not. In the text, their authority is not as effective as Jesus. Despite the tradition, it was nothing before Jesus. It is because it is out of the original way. It is believed that only the knowledge and status of oneself are made, and the authority is made a tool to accumulate only their interests.

On the surface, they were studying and teaching the law, but rather exploiting the traditions and positions they had established in advocating for themselves. No matter how much they cry out to the law, no one would be moved by the law. It was only accepting it intellectually and making only another authoritarianism.

The law is for the purpose of God. However, if it is not for God's purpose but for oneself purpose, it is changed.

HE RESTORES TRUE AUTHORITY IN TIMES OF LOSS OF AUTHORITY.

It was an era when authority was lost. Today, there are countless experts in our society, such as scholars of the law of Jesus. They point out their own expertise. Even if you have a doctorate, only one field is the doctor, and you do not know anything else in other fields.

Numerous experts on the ground state their expertise. And they proceed to accomplish their work. The problem is when things have not been accomplished. If you do not achieve it, you will be frustrated and compete with other professionals to get inferiority.

According to our society today, when we look at the number of suicide deaths, there are more social leaders and experts than people who died because of poverty. A poor man is holding his life as if he is struggling to live somehow. However, those who have accumulated a certain degree of status are desperate and give up because of their limitations. The true authority must be respected and influenced by many. It must be the authority to build people. Jesus was the one who established the true authority in times of lost authority.

THE AUTHORITY OF JESUS

When Jesus was teaching, a man with a demon suddenly heard Jesus say, and went out to him, causing a seizure and shouting. "Why are you interfering with our work?" This is not the word of a man, but the word of demons that works in him. The demons also yielded before the authority of the word of Jesus.

They accepted the authority of Jesus as they were subduing demons in Jesus' command. The word of God that Jesus proclaimed was the very word of power that freed all men from the forces of the devil. The words taught by the scribes did not have authority to cast such demons. There was no history in the authoritarianism they put forward. But Jesus was different.

In our lives today, evil spirits exert tremendous power. The essence of demons makes a man obsessed with an evil spirit. That is the purpose of the devil. The devil keeps the man from believing in God. The devil does not want to give into the authority of God. We must have spiritual discernment to discern evil forces. Today, when we look at our society, people seem to be captivated by something. We can not defeat it with our strength. Man is a sinner from the beginning. If you do not believe in Jesus, you have no choice but to carry your sins for life.

So we have limitations. If we were to be able to do it by our own strength, all sicknesses would have been treated in our society long ago. We would have been living in a problem-free society. However, it is impossible to solve it by the power of man because it is done by evil. To truly repair this land, Jesus' authority must be restored. The authority of Jesus, who had surrendered with trembling with fear, should be restored again.

The Word of Jesus must be proclaimed in us and in our society. In order for our children to defend and overcome this generation, Jesus' authority must rule over their children.

Jesus is now with us in the spirit of truth. He is coming to the Holy Spirit of Comforter to help us. There is only one place where the wicked devil could fall down from this world. The devil has tempted all men to this day. Beginning with Adam and Eve, we have opposed so many people in human history so far. But the only thing that did not break down is the saints and churches with Jesus Christ.

In the history of mankind, it has not been destroyed by persistent Satan attacks. Why? It is because of the fear of Jesus. The demon feared Jesus. Even if the devil hears Jesus, it runs away. The devil can not touch the saints who believe in Jesus. The devil goes away not because of me, but because of Jesus Christ in me. We have to obey to the authority of Jesus living with the Spirit of Jesus in me.

A wise man is one who does not grieve the Holy Spirit. Jesus is the one who can free us from evil power. There is the authority in that ability.

{Meditation Point}

1) Have you been jealous rather than learning and following rather than looking at the merits of someone who does not have me?
2) Where does the spiritual authority to win this age come from?

CHAPTER 8

RECEIVE CLEANLINESS!

Luke 5: 12-16

"Jesus reached out and touched him. I am willing, he said, be healed! And instantly the leprosy disappeared (Luke 5:13)."

THE LORD takes off our filthy clothes. And He puts on new clothes. A new garment is a cloth made of the faith of Jesus Christ. Cloth tells us what kind of person he is. Athletes wear sportswear in the stadium. Soldiers wear military uniforms and students wear school uniforms. It is a formal dress. What clothes should the Christian wear? It is the clothing of Christ. People are tired of life. They need a help. They live in the world.

It is exposed to temptation. The world tries to put on other clothes for the people, the clothes of the world, the clothes of the substance, the clothes of power, the clothes of the uncleanness, and so on. The people who have lost the judgment of faith are going to wear any clothes among them.

They try to wear clothes that are packed incorrectly. What does the Lord say? He says to take off clothes of sin and be holy. And to restore the lives of the people, who are dressed in the garments of God's grace. The clothes of the poor are old and separate. Those who sit on the street begging, look at our neighbors who desperately need help. Their clothes tell their situation. The Lord strips off the folks who are underground and clothe them with clothes of faith. We must come before the Lord.

The burden of unclean sin, the clothing of sin, must be lifted off and a life of sanctification must be lifted. A leprosy patient is a figure of a forsaken people of that era. The life is terrible. No matter how clean the clothes are, it gets dirty again due to the wound. The appearance of a spiritual leprosy patient, the appearance of patients with leprosy in the body is similar. The Lord heals from the wound and restores their lives. He restores the life of the people by cleansing.

ILLNESS OF LEPROSY FOR JEWS

The Jews regarded leprosy as a curse of God. A leprosy patient was an unclean person who could not live with normal people. So they lived outside the village where they were isolated from the social community. Mostly they came down to town and lived to beg, and when exposed to the common people, severe persecution was given to them. Even formal gatherings, as well as occasions with people, have lived a lonely life without being able to participate. In the Bible, the leprosy patients tell them that they are lepers as follows: First, they have to clothe and loosen their hair.

Second, they should cover their upper lip with hands and shout "Tame, Tame". So people had to listen to the sound first and avoid it first. Tamera means "I am an unclean person." The act of covering up the upper lip is a self-deprecating existence, and it is an expression that thoroughly depreciates itself. They could not be with other people, they had to live lonely.

Through leprosy, we can learn about the nature of sin. Sin causes the normal appearance of a person to be distorted. Sin always has a distorted appearance.

It is not normal. It is a sin that is always distorted. If a man sinned, he could see his mind changing. He does not look at the world with normal eyes. Sin always loves to hide. It hates to be exposed. Leprosy symbolizes sin in the Bible. That is because it has the characteristics of sin. It could not come into the camp with the tabernacle, which is always the symbol of God's presence.

Nowadays leprosy is able to inhibit the onset by moderate medication and can live almost normal life. However, leprosy at that time had no cure. The onset meant death. This is also like sin. The wages of sin is death. If you sin, you will soon die. If we do not believe in Christ and become children of God, we can not escape death by sin. The Saints do not receive condemnation in eternal judgment through Jesus, the way to live eternally.

Sinners are lonely. Satan steals people thoroughly. If you sin, the moment is sweet. It is because of the sweet temptation of sin. But more and more, as you enter into the bosom of sin, the more you enter, the more you become a sinner like addicting to drugs and eventually turn your body into the hell.

Sin isolates us from God and isolates us from people. In order for us to make a fresh start as a spiritual child, we must solve our sin problem. You can not live on as a spiritual leprosy patient.

WHAT ARE THE WISHES OF THE LEPERS FROM THE TEXT?

He wanted to live like a human being. Once he was free from this leprosy, he was eager to live in harmony with others without being isolated and not being bullied as he fell in love with others. However, people's reactions were always cold. He did not even tolerate coming near. In the end, the lepers ask the Lord for help. "If you can, Lord, I want to be cleansed." He prays before the Lord. There would have been many lepers at the time. But only one of them wanted to be healed of his illness.

So he comes to the neighborhood where access is prohibited and he is appealing. He wanted to get a fresh start from the disease that had plagued him in the past.

The man who had leprosy all over his body wanted to live a new life now. Anyone new to starting is important. Anyone who wants to change their life into a new life through Him must now come before Him with our shameful past. We must know that there is only one God, not a man, who will take away those who have been blasphemed because of their sins.

Jesus heard the wish of the lepers. And now how does he fix the lepers? He handed him directly and healed him. Others just fixed it with a word. No, he did not go to the scene directly, but he fixed it with the word. But this case is different. He touched the body and healed it. What does this mean? People made leprosy unclean and far away. They hated getting close to them. But the Lord was different. The others did not get close, but the Lord approached. And He touches.

Jesus is the one who touches my heart. I am the wounded person who comforts my heart and touches me directly. This means that He knows me best.

It means that He knows who I am and what kind of pain I have. Nobody can comfort the wound. Someone should touch it. Just as

Jesus touched the body of the lepers, our Lord today wants to touch me. And he says: "I want to be cleansed!" Just as I want to be clean, the Lord also means that I desperately want to be cleansed. He is the Lord who knows me best. The illness of the lepers was cleansed.

THE WORD OF THE LORD

He does not tell anyone that he has been healed first.

Then he went to the priest to show himself, to prove that he was clean, and to give an offering as Moses commanded.

The ceremony of cleansing proceeded in the first and second. The first was made through ceremonies designated outside the camp by priests. And officially declares that it has become clean.

Secondly, it is conducted in the tabernacle inside the camp. The priest offers four sacrifices for the lepers. The symbols used in the cleansing ceremony are living sacrifices symbolizing that the lepers are freed from all diseases and uncertainties.

A lush cedar symbolizes infinite vitality that overcame the disease of death. And the scarlet thread symbolizes the recovered color (blood color). The hyssop is symbolic of the painful illness of the illness leaving and being healed.

The lepers are officially recognized as having been cleansed of all sins, no more unclean in the eyes of many, through the cleansing ceremony.

Jesus cleansed the lepers and gave them care not to be rumors. Usually, good things are worth of rumors. But Jesus did not give a rumor. The reason for this can be seen by looking closely at the text. Jesus did not first give a rumor but to visit the priest. Why? It means to show the priest that people are clean, obedient, and changed. It means to prove to the people that the former sinful body has been sanctified and transformed into a holy people. If it is cleansed, people will acknowledge him, and it is a testament to Jesus' work.

This is a very important word for us as God's people. Where can I find evidence of my being born again and changed? It means that I can be found in my changed behavior. Everyone who met the Lord was transformed into a blessed life.

All the stinking sins are forgiven and filled with the joy that the Lord has given me. My sin problem was solved. I am born again to God, and people know that God is living through my transformation, and because of this, Jesus is naturally communicated.

As the lepers were healed, more and more rumors spread about Jesus, and numerous people gathered to be healed of their illness. At this time, Jesus quietly withdrew and prayed in a quiet place. Many things ahead, Jesus did not neglect his prayer life.

{Meditation Point}

1)What is the pain of sin? So far, what method did people use to solve their sin problem? (Buddhism, Confucianism, Hinduism, Islam, etc.)
2)What should I do to start a new start in the Lord? What can I do to meet the Lord who wants to touch my wounds in my life?
3)What was changed before I believed in Jesus and after I believed in Jesus?

CHAPTER 9

FAITH IN OVERCOMING DISABILITY

Mark 2: 1-12

"So I will prove to you that the son of man has the authority on earth to forgive sins. Then Jesus turned to the paralyzed man and said, stand up, pick up your mat and go home (Mark 2:10)."

WHAT YOU should know [The roof of Israel]: It is not so difficult to make holes through the roof at this time.

The roof of Palestine was a structure that could rise to the roof easily because of the stairs outward. And the roof was flat, and the wooden pillars were used as the framework, and the straw was weaved in it, and it was filled with earth again. The piercing of the roof is the removal of the soil and the straw and the plank to make a hole. Anyone was able to get rid of the roof.

There is a person we should meet today. He is a patient who does not behave like a paralytic disease. It is someone who can not move without help. It was not self-reliant and life was always dependent. He decides to go to the Lord with the help of his friends. People should live on each other. You should not live independently. We should live together sharing sociality. A person who is alone becomes lonely. No one is with you. In a lonely loneliness, w can not get out of the corner of dark life.

The people become the will of each other when they are two, not one. The paralytic who is lying in the seat is no longer alone because there are friends who can cry together and share the pain. There is a desire that he can get out of bed only to the fact that he has a friend. Friends lead him to the Lord. The people are united to come to meet the Lord. When we become one, we have strength and comfort. In such a group of people, the grace and blessings of the Lord come upon them.

JESUS WITH THE POWER OF GOD

Galilee was in one village witnessing the word. No matter where you go, Jesus is always crowded with people around Him. In the place where the Word was witnessed, the Jews and the teachers of the law and the Pharisees from all Jerusalem sat together and listened to the word. The reason why they heard the word was that they did not come out of their hunger for the word of the Lord but kept their place to accuse Jesus of any violation of the law. The two categories to listen to at that time were the one they listened to and heard (the people) and the other one they listened to as the Pharisees. Jesus did not conscious these. It was not the Pharisees who had not noticed and watched.

There was no shaking in Him. If you are like a regular person, you would not have been able to witness the word properly because you were atrophied before those who came to accuse you. But Jesus was different. He was proud to witness the Word because he had confidence and faith in the Gospel. And above all, Jesus had the ability to heal disease.

Jesus is the Son of God and the God of power to heal all diseases. The Pharisees could not repair the disease anyhow, because there is no love in their hearts and always full of condemnation. There is no history there. The ability to heal, just like Jesus, means that he loved those poor souls. So, people are driven to hear the Word around Jesus.

THOSE WHO CAME BEFORE THE LORD

Four people come out of a paralytic. It does not mention the process of bringing a paralytic to the sick, nor the relationship between the sick and four people.

However, when we look at the context of one text, we can see that the sick and four people were in close relationship, because at that time the sick man was condemned as a sinner by the unclean. The normal person was reluctant to contact the sick.

Nevertheless, these four people had contact with the paralytic, which had also come on the stretcher to the Lord. Perhaps they knew each other and were friends. They could not pretend that the rest of the people just saw a friend suffering. Therefore, they believe that

Jesus will be able to heal a friend's illness at the end of the sentence, and they took him with discomfort in love with his friend. We have one thing to realize here. It is to keep the righteous as a friend. A friend who can only be prosperous can not be a true friend. They understood him very well as a friend.

He is a true friend who is in trouble and in difficult times. The family did not come with a paralytic. It came with the person and those close to him. They transcended the law. It was love. They were willing to devote themselves to their friends with a loving heart. Because that mind was ahead, they saw a lot of people and did not give up, but they found a way to go to Him.

It is difficult for one and four people to go through the crowd to Jesus. They did not give up. They found the way. They looked for the way. It was the way to break through the roof and bring the sick to Jesus.

The act of seeking the way of four people to the Lord can be seen as an act of prayer in some way. Prayer makes our actions active. Do not give up a prayer. Prayer makes a way to find the way and go on its way. Prayer is not disappointed or discouraged by any obstacles in front of us. They were actively searching and asking for the road that was not there.

Jesus saw their faith. He has seen the faith that does not give up, faith that actively goes to the Lord, and faith that loves the sick.

When they testified of the Word, they were puzzled by the sudden appearance of the scene, but Jesus praised their faith. And he declared the remission of sins in his place, "Little man, your sins are forgiven." A little grown up does not mean a little person. The little ones here are humble. The psychic is hungry. He is a desire for grace. There are those who just come out of the chapel. You should not get out of your mind.

The attitude of mind in the chapel is low mind. He is the one who comes before the Lord in the spirit of longing for the grace of God. The grace of God is upon such a person. Point to such a person and say in another Bible, "Son! It is the child of God." Now point to the paralytic and the four men, Son! The Lord said. The whole relationship with God has been restored. The remission of sins means that the sick is a sinner.

A man has sinned and the disease has come in return. The word Jesus forgives for sin means healing the sick. When we receive forgiveness of sins, we become children of God.

"Who purchased our freedom and forgave our sins" (Colossians 1:14). It is a wonderful blessing for those who desire God's grace, and who see Him, as His children. Jesus shed water and blood on the cross for this purpose. It is to make us better.

THE REACTION OF THE PHARISEES AND SCRIBES

There were people who had different thoughts on the miracle scene. They were Pharisees and scribes. They were thoroughly rejecting Jesus. They were looking for a complaint to accuse Jesus of the day rather than sitting there and receiving his grace. They were hard-hearted.

If you have a hard heart, no matter how good you give it, you can not hear it. They were scribes. How many words have you lived? He recited the word from his childhood. He would have read and read the Word to get his ears stung. There was only the Old Testament at that time. All the contents Jesus taught in the synagogue witnessed a new gospel with the content of the Old Testament. The Pharisees and the scribes knew what they already knew and could not accept the Word properly. So they could not tolerate the words and actions of Jesus. Rather, they tried to kill Jesus by denouncing him as a priest.

The Word should not be taken as a head as knowledge. Then the mind becomes hardened. And he speaks. "Why do you think about this in your mind?" Why should you interpret it as such a doubt? In verse 9 Jesus says that he also has the power to forgive sins and has the power to heal the sick. Jesus means to have the power to do either of these two things. In the Bible, Jesus actually does both. He proclaimed forgiveness of sins to Zacchaeus, and remission of sickness and remission of sins to the paralytic.

There are many other examples. Jesus can forgive sin with his word and heal the sickness. Jesus is the one who does both. Today He does both. First, he declared forgiveness of sins. A paralytic is a person who can not move because of his limbs. He can not take things by hand or walk. Then he told the sick person to take a seat and walk. He did not say to his friends to raise him up. He put his legs on the ground and told him to stand up. As he stood up and walked among the crowds without going up to the roof with the statue, many people saw the sight and glorified God.

He is the one who surprises us. The Lord is speaking equally to us. He asks us to stand up and walk. We do not live a life dependent on others and says to live independently. And He wants everyone to see our change. And he wants to glorify God through us.

I hope this history will be full of us.

{Meditation Point}

1)We are people who testify of the Word. Have you been bored because of the environment around you and have not boldly witnessed the secrets of the gospel? What about our attitude to hear the Word?
2)How much did we pray for our friends who live with us? And with what heart do you come before Him?
3)Do you have anything else that makes me dependent on you like a paralytic disease? The Lord tells us to come to our place directly.

CHAPTER 10

HANDS RESTORED

Luke 6: 6-10

"He looked around at them all, and then said to the man, stretch out your hand. He did so, and his hand was completely restored (Luke 6:10)."

THE OLD Testament Sabbath begins on Friday night. The Jewish law says so. But the New Testament Sabbath is Sunday. The Lord's Day is the seventh day a week. It is the day that the Lord was raised from the dead. It is a blessed day that breaks all the powers of death.

The resurrection of the Lord is the day of life. The saints come to God on Sunday and receive spiritual life. It is the day anyone can enjoy in the name of Jesus. There is a person to meet in the Word. He is a man whose hands are dry and can not do anything. Hands are important among the functions of the body. I hold my hand and work.

It can be said that the hands have dried up is like having lost the place of life already. When the hands are dry, it means that they no longer have the ability to produce. Where in the people's life, is the miserable situation of poverty? All the livelihoods were cut off, and the people who had been living with their hands were living like the underside of which they did not reap. The Lord heals him on the Sabbath day and restores the meaning of the Sabbath day. The Sabbath is the day when a poor people come to the Lord to help. It is the day of experiencing the infinite possibility that the life is not dependable but can happen by the power of oneself.

The people will do much with the help of the Lord. They get up, work, and glorify God.

WHAT IS THE SABBATH DAY?

Jesus did not break the law of the Sabbath but rather restored the law of the Sabbath. The word recovery here does not mean that it breaks down all existing things and makes something completely different. The restoration that Jesus said means that he has acknowledged the existing things and supplemented them to perfection. Jesus perfected the meaning of the Sabbath day. So far, people have mistakenly thought about the Sabbath.

They misunderstood the true meaning of the Sabbath he intended. The Jews did not do anything on the Sabbath day, nor did they love the lawful. So they made a Sabbath without touch, a Sabbath without joy. Rather, this has become a big curse for people. Condemnation and judgment and formal worship dominated the Sabbath.

Originally God's intentions made the Sabbath day a true day of rest and peace for man. On the Sabbath, and in God, we obtain a real rest, peace, and return with new strength. It is the Sabbath day that glorifies God. So the Lord of the Sabbath is the Lord. On the Sabbath day, our Lord comforts the Word with all the saints who worship and gives us peace. We experience God's presence and life on the Sabbath day. The Pharisees, however, have made the Sabbath itself a form of ordinance and ritual without joy by making various regulations.

The Sabbath is not a day of death. The Sabbath is a day of joy and thanksgiving. It is Sabbath day to worship God. The owner of this Sabbath is Jesus. Jesus resurrected the concept of the Sabbath day. The day that overcame the power of death is the Sabbath and the Sunday.

This week, which is celebrated every week, is, therefore, correct even if it is the resurrection week. The meaning of the Easter Sunday is once a week. We must prepare the day and wait for the Lord to be filled with the joy of resurrection. Even if we keep the Lord's Day well, our faith will grow.

Even if we just keep worshiping God every week, we can survive the resurrection faith. Those who do not have the faith of resurrection have no joy.

But it is the only blessed day in which the Lord is suffering and resurrected for me, and is the only blessed day in which we can live in the world and comfort our suffering.

JESUS AS THE LORD

On the Sabbath day, Jesus enters the synagogue. The reason for entering the synagogue is to teach. He wanted to serve with the Word. There was a man with one hand in the synagogue. When one hand is dry, it means that the hand is deformed to such an extent that it can not be used. It is not the same size or length as the other hand. It means that the hand is broken and can not move. For some reason, he can not tell if his hands are dry. However, these days, there would be many reasons why the body was born with a physically deformed body or that the hand was dry in an accident with illness.

What should be noted is that he could not move his hands. Hand plays an important role in the body. The role of the hand is crucial in the realm of life, when you eat, or when you write. If your hand is uncomfortable, you can not do anything. It is not as easy as the hands do, though the feet can take over. In another Gospel, the hand was called the right hand.

Most right hands have more functions than left hands. This right hand was dry, so it would have caused many inconveniences in living. He was ashamed to be exposed to others. In some ways, this dry hand was a great shame for the man.

There will be some shameful parts to us as well, like these hand dry ones. How good is it to be as normal as others? How good would it be for others to live in the same healthy body? But it is not. The hand is in the most visible position in the body. Such a hand was twisted, so it would have looked grim. What do you think of me if you know my shame? Perhaps it would have made a lot of noise, and it would have been a big hurt to be prone to be pointed, ignored, and sometimes pitied at the same time, "That man has got his hands dry because he made a mistake!"

Jesus saw a poor man crouching at the corner of the synagogue, unable to show him in the presence of others. And by setting him in front, He wanted to show people what day of the week was and what he should do for God. Jesus was not conscious of the eyes of people, especially the eyes of the Jewish religious leaders. He did not notice them. Jesus, who was always in front of all the people, called the man who was boldly handed in front of the leaders who spied on that day to accuse him and said to come out in the middle.

Do not hide anymore. For as long as he felt shame because of his shameful past, he told me not to live as if he were a sinner. He stands firmly among the people.

And he set him up in the middle, and he continued to speak. "Which is right on the Sabbath day to do good things, to do evil things, to save lives, or to kill?" He said so much. It is right to do good things, save lives. It is something that everyone ought to do. However, until now people have noticed that religious leaders have not been able to do that while watching the public. For good works, you should not observe human perception. If this is a good thing for the gospel and it is for others, it is also in harmony with God's heart. God is good and love. It means that what I do is to save a life, and to benefit others, that will be in harmony with the will of God. We often ask about God's will. Where is God's will? What is God's plan for me? I often question.

At that moment we want to make a good judgment. There is a standard of right judgment. First, is it for my glory or for the glory of God? The God who is in me must be acknowledged. Second, is it for good? Good work, blessed work, good work for others is what God wants. He will give joy to all by his choice, and if it is a joyful thing, it is God's pleasure. Such work should be done without seeing the people.

Jesus also wanted to clarify the standard. So far, it was not acceptable to heal the sick on the Sabbath. The leaders did not accept it. So they thought it was God's will that they would not heal those who suffered from the disease on the Sabbath. Good work warms people's hearts. They are in the middle of difficulty and sued while looking at it. If you have people who think you are already a person who is far from the will of God. There is no such cruel act as saying that people are born to live like this for a man whose hands are dry, and who is cursed for the rest of his life. It is the same as killing that person. The more people with such an evil mind, the harder it becomes to live in this world.

Jesus asks us not to live that way. He tells them to be pleased even in the life of faith. He understands more and loves to live. Ask the leaders to look around the synagogue once. Who is there to find out who is sitting in that corner with an unexplainable pain?

Jesus said to them in verse 5 that their hearts were grieving and angry with hardships for those who could not have one. Jesus came to Jerusalem on Palm Sunday and went into the temple and became angry with the shopkeepers who made the temple a marketplace. Woe is full of righteousness. It is anger that can not endure what is wrong, unrighteous. And Jesus told him to reach out. Many people were watching. And he stretched out his bent hand. He restored it. He is the one who opens all the bands of our lives. It gives my heart out of the broken heart because of the wound. He is the one who comforts you to live dignifiedly.

Those who want to come to this Lord and be comforted must first come out, even if they put aside other things on Sunday. You must come to hear the word. It is good to come and have a corner. Second, we must stand in the middle. I must now ask my disgrace now before the Lord, that I should heal you. Third, we must live with love. We have to understand. Did he do that? How long have you been in the synagogue? He should be born. We must go under the cross of Jesus. If you raise your sick hand, the Lord is the one who heals you.

{Meditation Point}

1)In what sense does Sunday come to me? In what way do I prepare for Sunday?

CHAPTER 11

WAITING FOR IS ALSO FAITH.

Matthew 8: 5-13

"When Jesus heard this, he was astonished and said to those following him, I tell you the truth, I have not found anyone in Israel with such great faith (Matthew 8:10)."

IN FAITH, patience causes the rich fruit of the Holy Spirit. Seeds sprinkled in the spring must wait until the harvest. Just as belief can not expect mature fruit from the seeds sown immediately, patience is a necessary process to bear fruit. Without patience, nothing can be obtained. Faith, love, and hope go through patience. We need patience until we serve and serve one person. The seeds of patience shown in my heart cause the fruits of patience to be made. Waiting is the best attitude of faith. We are waiting for the Lord to touch and train us. This waiting does not mean passivity. It is our active response. We will wait. It means not to wait but to actively pursue waiting.

Therefore, there must be hope in waiting. Hope is not only our wish but a living hope for the Lord. We hope the Lord will respond to our expectation. What is the true figure of the people in Christ?

Now, there is nothing but helplessness, but someday you will be strong and willing and waiting until you have the appearance of the people as the most popular people until the Lord's true discipleship. The people are waiters who waiting for the Lord's time, waiting for their time. We find the people waiting in the picture of the Roman centurion.

He is a leader and a man of power. In the meantime, he can see the people. He does not abuse his position. Rather, he relies on the Lord who does not have the power of the world. The centurion is modest. The humility is the best religious character of the people.

ROME CENTAUR POSITION

At that time, the centurion was a soldier stationed under Roman rule. He was a Gentile, an invader, a Roman soldier, or a mercenary soldier. He is a commanding officer with about 100 soldiers stationed in Capernaum. The centurion's power is as strong as the rock.

He was a man who had no fear in the world. At that time, the most popular job was to become a soldier. It was a time of great honor to be promoted as a soldier, to have a high rank.

As a favorite soldier, as a successful man, the centurion had a warm heart. He did not tell anyone. He doesn't have discrimination. It was a wide-minded person who treats people freely and does not teach by oneself by having things. His servant's body got sick. The servant was an asset. It was nothing. The life of the servant was like the life of a fly. But the centurion was not like them. The centurion did not think of man as his own. He saw a human as a precious being. The centurion had no cruel personality that could be found in the soldiers. It was not cold either. It was a person full of humanity.

Through the personality of the centurion, we look at ourselves. How do we treat people today? I must use that person for me. Do you treat it as? Or does it really give me for treating and loving someone to love? According to another Bible, the centurion is said to have done many good things beyond the nation. He has built a synagogue for the Israelites and has done many good works. He had a broad and loving heart that we should follow. The words of praise have changed people. The centurion did not ignore the species. He was recognized as a personal nobleman. Such a mind has saved the life of the servant.

CENTURION'S HEART

The centurion had faith.

It was not a theoretical or doctrinal belief. It was the same experience that he experienced in his life.

He is a soldier and a bold man. Boldness means courage. It is the courage to be ahead of the soldier who is not afraid to be afraid and does not shrink any situation or environment. As a Gentile and Roman soldier, he hears rumors about Jesus and rumors of his healing power. And he was convinced that he would fix a servant. Jesus is convinced that he is the Messiah sent by God and has made up his mind to go to Him.

There was humble.

The work of faith produces miracles. However, all those who experienced miracles were people who lowered themselves. The Bible tells us that God is far from the proud and that he is near the humble. So much lowering oneself before the Lord means to be a valuable shortcut to experience the work of faith.

He went out to the elders of the Jews and defended him. The centurion acknowledges the centurion that, despite its high status, he did not intend to repress the Jews, but even to serve the Jews. Those who humble themselves are also acknowledged by men. The centurion seems to lower himself in front of Jesus.

In verse 6, Jesus was chosen by many to seek the healing of the centurion's servant. And he is going to the house, and the centurion sends his friends and says, "Lord, do not labor until you come to my house. Our house is so unbearable that we can not have the Lord." It is not an excuse for taking the Lord. He who was a mighty power and rich man did not see the Lord with the eyes of the world.

The centurion saw the Lord as the great Son of God, as a prophet, as a measure of salvation. He healed the sickly, cast out demons, and acknowledged God as God who witnessed the gospel of the kingdom. So he could not afford to take Him home. This is like the confession of Peter. Peter found himself before Jesus. Beyond his common sense, Jesus came to Christ as Christ. When Peter knew of Jesus' existence, he knew he was a sinner. The centurion is the same. In front of Jesus, he realized that I am a small person, a sinner.

And he believed that Jesus could fix the sick only from a distance. So he said humble, "Just say the Lord. Then you will heal my servant."

He who stands before the Lord of light is bound to be humble. We are still proud because we have not met the Lord properly. It rejects the light of the Lord. So the grace of the Lord flows down like water. He gives grace to the humble. He saves the humble. Job 22:29 "God saves the humble." In Proverbs 3:34, he said, "Truly, he laughs at the arrogant and gives grace to the humble." The centurion longed for grace and met the Lord of Light.

There was a waiting faith.

Faith is also waiting. We feel like it will be done right away if we pray. And we hope to get something as soon as possible and get something done. We hope that history will take place right away. A true attitude of faith requires patience for waiting. It is a hasty posture to think that the seed will be sown right away and the fruit will be harvested the next day. If you sow, you have to wait until it buds. And wait for the weather. You have to wait until the fruit comes out. Our beliefs also require an attitude of sowing seeds rather than visible fruit. If you sow the seeds, you will be able to bear fruit in our next generation even if it is not my generation. Even if it is not me, someone else can harvest the seeds of my seed. You have to wait. We have to wait until the end. We have to wait for someone and wait for when we stand up.

We must wait as Abraham waited until the age of 100 to get Isaac. Samuel grew up and was trained in the temple until he became an adult and became a leader. David was trained to wait until he became king, and Moses waited 80 years before becoming the leader of Israel. Work is not done without preparation. Miracles do not happen.

The centurion did not tell to come to his house right now. Lord, I will hear from you. I will wait for my servant to heal. I will have faith and obey the Word without any doubt.

The centurion, as a soldier, is in the position of a soldier and is awaiting orders from his superior. A soldier should not act till the boss orders and directs. Each soldier is ordered not to take orders from his superior.

The soldier, the centurion, waited in obedience to the command that Jesus had spoken. We have not heard the voice of God because our voice is greater than the voice of God. My experience is more important and assertiveness is more important. This is an act of distrust.

If I really believe, I have to be a wait-and-ready person. Do not doubt that you should have faith in God. Such faith is the belief that is praised by God.

{Meditation Point}

1)In what way do we treat people? I want you to look back whether or not you are evaluating by the outside of the person.
2)Do you have a special prayer topic?

CHAPTER 12

LET'S RAISE A YOUNG MAN.

Luke 7: 11-17

"The dead man sat up and began to talk, and Jesus gave him back to his mother (Luke 7:15)"

PEOPLE WHICH means populace are always alive. The spirit of the people continues to live again. They don't compromise with injustice. They don't rely on authority or flattery. They do not turn away the poor.

They are those who are in circumstances that are worse than they are compassionate and helpers. The mind of the people is that of the youth. Young people do not depend on biological age. His heart is like a young man, righteous, rich and generous, and biologically, he is a young man even in his old age. The Lord awakens and sets up youth of this age. Heal the old and diseased heart and restore it to the young man's heart.

Why did He do that? It is because Jesus himself is a young man.

He is the most active minister for the kingdom of God in His thirties. Always look for people, talk about problems, and solve them. He moved the longest distance at his youngest age, and he had dozens of times at times dangerous in his life. He lived more youthfully. The Lord wants the people of this age to live like a youth. However, the young man who is supposed to live like that in the Word is lying dead in the coffin. A young man in a coffin is a helpless people who can not do anything. The ministry that raised the people from the dead is the Lord's great and wonderful work.

JESUS' THREE MIRACLES

In the Gospels, many miracles of Jesus are recorded. But there are three miracles. This miracle is the miracle of delivering the dead from the grave. 1) Raising the son of the widow (7: 11-17) 2) Raising the daughters of Jairus the synagogue (8: 40-56) 3) Raising Martha and her brother, Lazarus. It is important to save the dead from the ministry of

Jesus.

The first is to give hope to those in despair by saving the dead. Death is a desperate situation. There is no hope. The power of death takes away joy from the remnant. Look at the Bible. It takes away joy from man. Even the will of life is lost. Jesus wanted to remind the desperate people that he was not alone because he saved the dead. He wanted not to be alone, but to realize that God is with us.

Second, the reason for saving the dead is that they believe in Jesus and that they will not die, but that they will have eternal life. When they see the dead in their eyes alive, they each look into Jesus in their hearts and have a desire that they will live again. The whole gospel was witnessed by the Lord. What is the Gospel? Listening is not enough. What did Jesus say when he called people? 'And behold,' he said. Do not listen with your ear, but actually come to the place and see.

Be clear in your eyes and confirm that Jesus is indeed the Lord of resurrection.

Do not think that seeing and experiencing is not necessarily faithless. Believing without seeing is blessed faith. But seeing and believing is also worthwhile.

One of the suspect disciples is Thomas. Thomas said that he would not believe himself without confirming Jesus' hands, feet, marks, and nail marks. So Jesus came to Thomas and showed his hands and feet so that Thomas believed in the risen Lord. Since then Thomas has trusted the Lord. He did more ministry than the other disciples. He survived to the end and went to India and witnessed the Gospel. He went farther than the other disciples, witnessing the gospel, building the church, and being martyred.

This is the reason why Jesus is taking his disciples to the resurrection of the dead so that the dead will not be afraid of death by seeing them live. He rose up the dead before them in order to have a bold mind before death.

JESUS COMING INTO HIS PERSONALITY

Jesus went to a place called Nain. Nain was about 20 kilometers from Capernaum. Jesus did not go alone when he was going to Nain. In verse 11 it was said that the disciples and the crowd were together.

Jesus knows everything. When he entered Nain, he knew that the mother of the dead had already been waiting there, and he went there. She wanted to save her son before he left. So, when he came to the place called Nain, he did not go alone, but with a lot of people. He was really close to the gates, and they came out with a dead young man. If a person dies, they must go out the gate. There was a place where people were staying there. This young man was also on his way out of the castle.

Talk about the identity of this young man. A young man is the only son of a mother. And the mother is a widow. She was out of the gates with many people in sorrow for losing her son. If a person turns 100 years old and passes away, it is a good mourning. How delightful would it be if he lived long and enjoyed living long lives? But this young man died young. He could not even see his peers and died. It was probably a little over 20 years old. For the widow, this son was the only hope. It was the will of life, it was all. In fact, this son should be seen to have lived to this day. If it were not a son, the mother had no meaning of life, and it was no different from a dead one. The widow no longer has the meaning of life without a son.

Jesus saw the widow coming out of the castle. In verse 13, Jesus tells them that he had compassion for a widow. And when he had compassion, he said not to cry. Jesus was God. God has mercy on the widow and the orphan of this world. In the Book of Deuteronomy, most say that they care about and care for orphans and widows. "After you harvest the vineyard of your vineyard, do not take it again, but leave it for the guest, the orphan, and the widow."Deuteronomy 24:21 The widows are the ones who have no place to depend. If people around you do not think about them, you have no choice but to live a lonely life.

Jesus also has mercy on the poor, especially the widows and the orphans who have no dependence on the gospel, so that he has done many miracles and comforted them. He has taken them into the arms of God himself. The Word tells us a little about the mind of Jesus. Jesus was a tearful man. He saw a lot of tears when he saw poor people. A lot of tears mean that love is abundant. When He saw the poor people, he did not just go by, but he always touched and treated their wounds. The Bible says that those who mourn will be comforted, and

JESUS ON THE SIDE OF THE WEAK

those who have mercy will be compassionate (Matthew 5: 4, 7). If the Son is dead and the sorrow is not comforted, there is no desire to live.

But Jesus not only comforts us with words but also makes the desperate situation a place of joy. He is the one who raises an amazing miracle in our lives. Jesus, touching the coffin, said, "Young man, I tell you, get up!" He is already dead. His ears are blocked, his mouth blocked, his body stiffened, and He said to rise up in a loud voice in front of the dead body.

When the word of the Almighty reached the dead body, the dead one sat up and listened, and he said. At that moment, the house was turned into a feast. Jesus gave her son to the mother after he died. The son of sadness will live as the son of joy and return to the mother's arms.

Those who were there were witnesses and those who watched the scene. It was not only one person but everyone who came out of the castle watched this moment of resurrection.

They glorified God. And each one confesses. "A great prophet has come among us." "God has turned to us." Rumors about Jesus who raised the dead were spread all over Judea and all around. Everyone is hearing the news of Jesus' miracles.

Today, this Jesus is the only hope of life for us. He is the one who raises me from the dead. He is the one who revives me in a desperate situation like death. Death is nothing. Just lie in the grave and wait for the body to decay. A young man lying in a coffin or a widow who is saddened by the loss of her son by the side can all be a figure of ours.

We must work in the midst and fulfill our mission and be a joy. There are many things to look for and a lot of missions. We can find lots of examples that our lives are often lacking. We can meet those who the body lived, but the thought and the will died. The mother is the same. She lived by looking at only one son. Looking at only one, the sadness has become bigger because one of them collapsed.

When things that they long for and depend on come down, people fall into the hell of despair at that moment. The things of the world that I depend on are things that can not be done and that will disappear someday. We must rely on hope. Spiritually dying I must be left in the hands of Jesus to live. Jesus must touch the coffin of death I am lying in. And listen to that voice.

Jesus calls my name and say; 000, Rise up! You must listen to the voice. In verse 15, Jesus says that he gave the young man back to his mother. What does this mean? It is said to have been all in the hands of the Lord until it comes to life.

The young man continued to be entrusted to the Lord as the Lord did. The Lord has done everything to get up, sit down and say. I hope that today we can become such a man that we are held in the hands of the Lord.

{Meditation Point}

1)Has the power of death ever crushed me? Was there a time when you wanted to die? Who do I have to depend on to win death?
2)What is my spiritual condition now? Who do I depend on? Is it the widow's reliance on the dead son? Or is it the Lord?

CHPATER 13

CALM DOWN.

Mark 4: 35-41

"He said to his disciples, why are you so afraid? Do you still have no faith?" (Mark 4:40)

ACCORDING TO historical records about Pompeii, it tells about the situation that was urgent at the time. Even if you see the artifacts from the Pompeii ruins in the past, you can see at a glance the situation that happened at that time. As soon as a volcano hits a huge city like a trap, the people in it are buried in the ash of the volcano.

In the middle of it, there are still fossils that have been eaten and danced, and men and women are enjoying it together and then buried and hardened like a hard stone. Some of the artifacts show that the moment the volcano hits the city, the people who came to the end in prayer.

WHAT DOES THE BIBLE SAY?

"Be careful of yourselves, that your hearts may not be turned backward by debauchery, vengeance, and everyday anxiety. And let that day not suddenly cover you like a trap, that day will come upon all who dwell on the whole earth." (Luke 21: 34-35)

No one knows his future. Everything in the world can be known on that day. One day I can tell how I lived.

When I walk through the world, I realize how I lived. Therefore a wise man is the one who prepares for a time to come someday before the moment of trial.

It is the hearts of the people not to panic when the people get troubled. And it is the people's mind that overcomes difficult times well. The Lord wants the people to prepare for the time and overcome with the Lord.

SAIL IN THE MIDDLE OF THE SEA.

In the midst of the night, He says to his disciples that he should go to
the sea. It is important when and where to go. It is time for the day to
fall. The night comes soon. But he wants to go to the sea at night. If
you are a regular person, do not sail at night. To go to the sea where
nothing is visible, you must take care of your life. Yet the Lord says to
go to the sea. It is because the Lord is.

If we do not depend on the Lord, we can not obey the Word.

The disciples went to the sea, obeying the word because the Lord went
with them. There are times in our lives. It is time for the night to come.
At that time, no one can predict. Suddenly, they come. The dark sea is
a miniature of our life. The climate that we meet at sea is changeable.
After being calm, it is again struck. It is the sea. There is a time when
the sea of this life we live in is calm but it is not.

We begin our voyage without anyone knowing the future. Christians
should not forget that the Lord is with them at such a time. At night,
the disciples could not predict the situation at sea.

The sky was dark and they could not see anything. They just went
to the sea as He said. If we knew in advance that a storm would soon
come, no one would have gone to the sea. It was in the dark sea. It was
dangerous. There was no bright light. Nevertheless, they planned the
sailing.

When you come to the center of the sea suddenly a big storm arose.
The waves hit the boat and pushed into the boat. The moment the
ship is filled with water. There is great confusion in the ship. People
seemed to be sinking, so they threw water out of the boat, and some
people tried to push out the water in the boat. A lot of people got
caught up in each other.

Until then they had forgotten that the Lord was with them in this
boat. They would obey his word and forget their first heart to the sea,
saying, "What would it mean for you to go out into the sea when the
day was gone?"

When there is a big trial in life, people forget what to do. We forget
to be with the Lord and try to solve the problem personally. They also
rinsed the water and threw everything into the sea. But that did not
solve it. The waves became rougher and the situation was getting

worse. Trying to solve it with their strength can make it harder to stand up.

Before we go out, we must find the Lord who is on the boat of life together. We must first understand who we are with. Sometimes it becomes more difficult if I forget that the Lord of Power is with me and try to solve my own problems. You must know the intention of the Lord who called me. We must first know why the Lord wants us to go to the sea tonight. We must know that Satan can not touch the Saints. We should not think that Satan allowed it when we met the difficult times of our lives.

Sometimes Satan shakes us, teases us, does not keep us quiet, but it can not sink us completely. Satan can not touch the Saints. If we can not do anything, I think it is because the demon is bothering me. But we should know that, rather than negative thoughts, we are living a precious opportunity to meet the Lord in the unstable life of the universe. The important thing is not the storm itself, but the Lord I must find in it.

LORD IN TROUBLE

When his disciples did not seek him, He was sleeping on a pillow. It was not a sturdy ship as it is now, and it was not a safe ship. It was only a piece of carving. The storm would have shaken the ship. Yet, in the shaking ship, He was sleeping with a pillow.

A similar situation arises if we do not seek the Lord. If we do not pray in trials, the Lord can not help us. How can you help me if I have not sought the Lord? If they can not do it, then they go after it and come back to the Lord with their two hands later up. How good would it be to find the Lord from the beginning? But if you can not do it yourself, then you are looking for the Lord. Luckily they were glad to find the Lord later. The prayer of the disciples awakening the Lord who sleeps in the boat can be called prayer in some way. The disciples, awakening Him, say: "Teacher, we are now dead. Why do not you take care of us? We pray. Lord! Look at me, and hear my prayer. If you are not Lord, there is no one to help me." Do not forget that prayer is the wisest person who seeks the Lord. Jesus awoke in the supplication of his disciples and rebuked for the wind.

And he said to the sea. Rewarding for the wind means that the power of the Lord has controlled things that weaken and frighten the faith of the disciples. Evil spirits say they can not touch the saints. Satan can test the Saints. But Satan can never bring down the Saints. The one who always wins is the Saints. The rebellion of the waves can be said to overthrow all elements of fear that weaken faith. The demon is not the objects to appease. It is an object to be rebuked and defeated.

Look at the shamans. I have never seen a shaman who scolds evil spirits. It is calm while meeting the evil spirits. That's not it. Evil spirits should be rebuked and defeated. It does not mean that the storm is the demon. It just means that we should be careful and alert to the evil forces that weaken the faith of the disciples using such a situation. And the Lord spoke to the sea. The sea is always there. Life was called the sea. So where is it that we can triumph over this life? It is the Word.

You must win your life with the Word. Let the sea be silent for the sea! Calm down! It is to be calm.

Do not cause any more waves, and do not give fear to the disciples. In the words of the Lord's power, the wind ceased and the sea became calm.

The Lord saw his disciples and said, "Why are you afraid? Why is there no faith? Do not be afraid, but be faithful." If you believe in the Lord, you will be able to protect yourself at sea. You have compassion on the disciples who were terrified by the waves.

The Lord has not promised that we will never face the terrible situation. In this world, a lot of storms are made. In an unexpected situation, a difficult situation is created and comes to the Saints. It also gives pain. This situation will not happen if you believe in Jesus. It should not be thought. Instead, the Lord wanted us to point out that whatever situation we face is greater than God, and that everything lies under his control. Therefore, the owner of a strong belief is someone who is convinced that even if he finds any terrible situation and harass the Saints, he will be able to believe in God's power and turn away his fear. We must realize that the word "prosperity" does not mean that there is no difficulty but that it means that even if some difficulty can be overcome, it can be overcome by the power of the Lord.

{Meditation Point}

1)When I was in the most difficult time, whom did I depend on?
2)When we meet difficulties, let's first look at what we have been trying to solve for ourselves without first finding the Lord and praying.

CHAPTER 14

LET OUT OF THE SNARE

Mark 5: 1-20

"For Jesus had said to him, come out of this man, you evil spirit!" (Mark 5:8)

THE PEOPLE are not the ones who are moved by their minds according to the values of the world. The people are the ones who are caught in the heavens. They are people who do not pay attention to the earth but live in the real kingdom of God. There was a mysterious crown. The person who wore this crown was a mysterious pipe in which the ambition in the mind of the person changed in the way of the crown.

Somebody used to have a crown and this crown became a helmet to protect the head when going to fight. Then the master of the crown says. "You like armed forces." When another person wore this crown, suddenly the crown turned into a greedy power for those who did it. Then the master said, "You are pursuing honor and power." Finally, when someone wrote this, suddenly the crown turned into a pure and humble man. The master then said to him, "You are a true Christian." What does this story tell Christians living in modern times? Many Christians follow Jesus and do not let their ambitions fall into their hearts.

People packaged in the name of Jesus are an unknown ambition. He wants to know his name in the name of Christians. Even those who minister to the Lord follow the values of the world as they follow them. This is all a snare. It is a snare set up in Satan's mind to entangle people. The people are wise. People are those who know what a snare to take off is. They are weak, heart clean, and longing for truth. They are the ones who bring a pure heart that can not be wrapped. People have different ways of living the world, but the important thing is that they live in a real Christian. Those who have no Lord in their hearts are those who are caught in a powerful snare. They have to get out of there.

Jesus Christ is the one who takes away the snare. The Lord said that He has the keys of David (Revelation 3: 7).

THE LIFE OF A DEMON-POSSESSED PERSON

He lived an isolated life.

This person lives alone. He could not do it with normal people. Before he was healed, he could not live with his family in a house with demons. The family also gave up on him. Because he could not live together in one family, he took him to the grave at the entrance of the village and stayed there. The devil makes isolation from people and frightening. Isolation can be said to be the result of terrible sin. This is the devil's favorite way. How miserable and pitiful is it? Isolation is a scary thing.

It is also a problem for those who have gone to the grave. They could not afford anymore, so they went to the grave. They will give up easily. It is like sending a man to a place like a grave to die.

He was arrested.

This man could not wear any clothes but was living in a snare like a beast. Here, the snare means the power of the devil. It is in a state of being captured by the devil. And people locked his chains and furrows to keep him from moving. No one had the power to control. This means the power of the devil. He can not break his chains and fences himself. It is the work of man. No matter how human beings try to control themselves, they do not. What does this mean? It means that there is a limit to what human beings can do. The snare of the devil can not be broken by human power. The Lord must come.

Only the Lord can escape from the snare of the devil. Satan still actively obstructs God's work. Satan then finds the target and puts a snare. The demons under the devil are as many as the army. I can not win. All are evil spirits devoured by the devil. The evil spirit comes to us as it turns into its own shape. And it makes the spiritual vision blurred and misleading. They know the Lord well. For these are also the creatures of God.

The Bible says that they are fallen one. It is not almighty. It is nothing before God's power. God will keep us safe from demons. On the last day of the world, all evil spirits will be thrown into eternal hell fire with Satan, the devil, the chief (Revelation 20:10).

He lived in self-oppressed (abused).

I did not consider myself honorable. We are God's creatures. It is the child of God. We do not compare anything in the world. We are delighted and pleased to see ourselves. But it is such a beautiful being that you do not see yourself beautifully. Selfishness is the abuse of self. It is too painful to abuse yourself. In v. 5, day and night, he was hurting his body with stone, screaming in the tombs or in the mountains.

The behavior of extreme people leads to this same behavior. Suddenly he loses his temper and hurts his body. He can not stand it. He has blood on his body but he does not feel pain. However, He can not stop this kind of life because it is already dominated by evil spirits. If you take your body with stone, you will not feel the pain.

Accept the pain as it is for granted. In a word, it has become chronic.

What is the name of this person?

The self is called an army. An army means that there are a lot of numbers. Actually, this young man's name is not an army. To speak of himself as an army must know that the evil spirit speaks for him. In other words, the demon in front of Jesus can be said to say his own identity. The demon must be seen as completely dominating this young man's thoughts and words. He then asks him not to drive him out of this region. Why are you asking this? This can be said to show the reality of evil as it is. He will stay completely among the people without going away and will continue to do evil. Evil spirits can still work in us. We should always stay at your side and look for a place to go.

Spiritual beings do not die. These evil spirits need a body to live in. This body does not care whether it is the body of a person or the body of an animal. While they were looking for a new body to live in, they finally saw a swarm of pigs passing by. That number was 2,000. It urges to let the nasty demons go into it. Jesus allowed it. Then a group of unclean spirits began to emerge from the body of a young man into the herd of pigs. Not one of them, but thousands of pigs. There are many demon-possessed people in the Bible.

Especially, Mary Magdalene was a woman with seven evil spirits. But this young man did more than this. There were countless numbers, not seven evil spirits. It is a word that shows how miserable this young man's life has been in the meantime. Nearly two thousand pigs are jumping into the sea at once. Witnesses who saw this incident by now became convinced that the power of Jesus overwhelmed demons. Since then, everything has been restored.

Especially when the young man saw his clothes are clean and he was sitting in a perfect mood, people even feared the Lord's authority. No one was able to control this young man, who had already been abandoned, and who knew that he would die because he had been abused for his life for the rest of his life. This event was as big an event as the case of saving the dead. Thousands of demons were nothing before the Lord's power.

The Lord controlled the power of demons at will. The demon can not stand the Lord. If this Lord is our Lord, we too can resist this evil power.

If there is absolutely what is necessary for Christians living in the world, it is to have the ability to win against the evil forces. The Lord gives such spiritual authority to all believers. Why am I falling over? You should not think about yourself, why are you weak?

The healed young man is now asked to stay with the Lord. He just wants to stay by the Lord and live as a disciple. But the Lord rejects it. There is a greater mission. The young man would have stayed by the Lord and would have wanted to be taught that the demon would not torment him again. However, he had already experienced a great ability. It is enough that he can live by witnessing the gospel.

As the Lord spoke, he went back to the family who had not been able to meet and witnessed the gospel. And he preached not only to his family but also to others. He was the perfect disciple of the Lord and used him as a testimony. He who encounters the Lord, who is overlaid with the power, changes all his life. In the past, he has become a lot of

people who can not do anything at all.
He who is helpless now becomes a complete winner.

{Meditation Point}

1)What is the result of sin? (isolation, bondage, self-oppressed)

(The result of sin: isolation, bondage, and self-oppressed) → (the power of Jesus Christ: liberation) → (evil forces retreat: victory) → (restoration: spirit, The Kingdom of God

CHAPTER 15

THE DAUGHTER OF JAIRUS
AND THE WOMAN WHO WAS HEALED

Luke 8: 46-56

"Then he said to her, daughter, your faith has healed you. Go in peace (Luke 8:48)."
"But he took her by the hand and said, my child, get up (Luke 8:54)."

NO COUNTRY will be accustomed to the word "wait" as Korea. Due to the geopolitical and historical interests of Northeast Asia, this land has been subject to the invasion of the powers, and it is also a hardworking country that has tried to protect the identity of the nation and keep its independence in the pockets of the great powers. In the wake of the Korean War, more than 90% of the country was re-emerged in the deserted wilderness, now in the G20, and the country as the model of the most successful nation in the world. All of this can be said to be the nationality that has been accomplished without waiting for the cord of hope. It can be said that the image of the Korean people is embedded in it. Opportunities come to those who strive for hope in this way.

There are two stories in the text. One is the case of raising the daughters of Jairus, the ruler of the synagogue, and the other is the case of a woman who has suffered from bleeding for twelve years.

Two stories may seem like different events, but the facts can be seen as a single event. Two events are recorded in the text, but the intention of the Lord is unified. It is the waiting and the power of the Lord. To those who wait, God is with us, and there is faith. There was a middle age between the Old Testament and the New Testament. The period of about 430years was a period of waiting and preparing for the Messiah, Jesus Christ.

During that period, the rebuilding and revival of the dynasties took place, and in the stronghold of the neighboring countries, the faith of the Messiah was to be kept as the last resort of the nation of Israel. In this way, waiting in God's history demands patience and hope. The people are waiters. It is not those who give up easily and have no tolerance, but those who wait for hope that new hopes will budge. We are the remnant of this land, the one who makes history through those who are on the side of God. A man named Jairus in the text and a woman who suffered from a woman's disease for 12years are just waiting and symbols of the people. Comfort is upon them that waits, glory in heaven, and great peace on earth.

THOSE WAITING FOR THE LORD

There were people waiting for Jesus to return. They were the followers of the Lord. They were those who had the hope of the kingdom of God, listening to the Word nearest to the Lord. These crowds followed wherever the Lord went. It was the people who talked about the Word of God on the mountain, and who kept the Lord's side in the synagogue while longing for the Word when teaching. There is no way to know what their name is or where they live. The important thing is that they waited for the Lord and the Word. To those who wait, God gives the Word and shows the events of miracles. Though they have no name and no light, but those who wait for the end, their faith is sprouting and growing in their hearts.

WHO IS JAIRUS, THE SYNAGOGUE RULER?

There was a man named Jairus, the synagogue leader. This man is literally the head of the synagogue. He was the man who prepared the synagogue and prepared to worship. The synagogue was the center of the life of the Israelites. The law was proclaimed, and it was a place to educate people. So the synagogue head had to be a man who knew the law. Those who knew the law at the time were trained in the Jewish tradition. Most of them did not accept Jesus as the Son of God because of the law. There were even those who were not proud and did not try to acknowledge others. The attitude of most synagogue rulers was arrogant, but Jairus from the text was different. He was interested in Jesus. And he was the one who recognized Jesus as the Son of God. Because he was such a person, he waited for Jesus to return. He waited with a prayer title. The prayer title was his daughter, who was just dying from sickness. The daughter was a great joy in the house. She was a pretty daughter who took on the love of her family while struggling with all kinds of troubles. But such a daughter is now in sorrow. If the daughter is sick, the joy is gone to the whole family. Even if only one person is sick in the house, the atmosphere of the house sinks heavily.

The nervous mood comes to the patient in a moody atmosphere. When his lovely daughter was dying, Jairus came to the Lord and begged me. Please come only once and ask for your daughter to pray. The Lord did not refuse the call of Jairus.

WHAT HAPPENED ON THE WAY TO JAIRUS'S HOUSE?

The Lord wanted to go to Jairus' house. On the way, a lot of people came to Jesus. All were people who flocked to see the Lord. Because there are so many people, one step could not move forward properly.

They were pushed and hit each other, and there was great disturbance among the crowd. But there is a new miracle work in it. A woman who has suffered from bleeding for 12years will come to the Lord and touch the Lord's skirt. Many people were pushing and pulling. But one of the many who was healed was a woman. As soon as she reached the cloth, her illness, which had been plagued for 12years, was clean.

No one knew that, but only Jesus and the woman knew. She knew that her sickness had improved as a party and that his power had disappeared from his body. Jesus wanted to know who had touched his clothes. And he called the crowd to confirm who she was. The woman could not hide the fact. Then she stood before the crowd to tell people why she had touched her hands and that she was clean.

She has testified before many people that she has solved the problem of her life that she could not solve even if she tried to take all medicines for 12years. Jesus looked dear to her faith. And he said, "Daughter, your faith has saved you, now go in peace." It is because of the woman's faith that the woman was healed. That faith saved her from the problems she was afflicted with in her life.

The woman stopped her way on the spot, and her illness was healed.

But because of this, one sad life is dead because of the delayed time. A worker at the house of Jairus, the synagogue ruler, comes to the scene and reports. Your daughter is dead and says you do not have to come anymore. In another Gospel, people speak to the Lord who has delayed his time. But the Lord said to them, "Do not be afraid; then the daughter will be saved." And when they come to the house, they go to the body of a daughter who is dead, with no one but three disciples and her parents alone.

The reason that no one was there was to put faith in those who were with them. Jesus tells us that the daughter is not dead, but is sleeping. People even laughed at the Lord, who had already expressed his resentment to the dead. Death was not the end of the Lord. Jesus raised the dead child by his hand and raised her up. Then the spirit of the child came back. What does the word spirit mean? When a person dies, the spirit escapes. The return of the Spirit means that this daughter is completely dead. But the Lord has called in the Spirit again. Jesus is the person who controls the life and death of man.

It is in the Lord's hand that we live and die. Likewise, the life and death of this daughter is also with the Lord. The Lord again brought her daughter from the grave. The Spirit returned and the child sat and rose and began to eat what he ate. The disciples who saw this scene together were amazed and her parents were more surprised. He wants to know that he who has raised the dead from among us has come to Jairus, the synagogue ruler, like the Word.

The Lord who heals a woman who has suffered from a chronic disease and frees him from the disease, and the Lord who raised the dead again, is the Almighty God who heals our sickness and gives eternal hope.

WHAT CAN WE REALIZE THROUGH TWO EVENTS?

It teaches us that it is important to wait when we pray. Jairus had to keep faith until the Lord came and not lose his desire for Him until the end. Everything is under the sovereignty of the Lord. People can think that the dying person is the first because Jairus wanted it first. The dying person rushed in first and thought that it was the order to watch this person first. In some ways, twelve years are not death sickness. It was not just hasty as it was just a disease. Nevertheless, the Lord did not go to the daughter who dies in part, but he healed this woman in the middle.

This is the difference between what the Lord thinks and what we think. The Lord is working more than we think. The power of the Lord, and His planning and works, also surpasses us. Therefore, you should not have grudging or complaining minds that you have a hasty mind and that you can not work.

On the Lord's side, there was nothing to do with the sickness or the illness that would not die or the order of the sickness. What the Lord wants is faith. So he said to the woman, "Your faith saved you." And to the family of Jairus, "Do not fear, but believe."

If we have a firm belief, we will not be shaken. No matter what the difficulties may be, faith can give us a great ability to hold the center of our lives. Those who have faith do not shake. And those who have faith can wait for the Lord's time.

Everything should be considered as a process. It is the Lord who knows my prayer title. And the Lord is the one who makes prayer answers. Until the answer is made, the Lord asks us to believe and sometimes to train us.

{Meditation Point}

1)Have you ever had an urgent mind while praying?
Let's think about the woman who waited for 12 years to be healed and the people of Jairo who could not wait any longer.

CHAPTER 16

IT SHALL BE ACCORDING TO YOUR FAITH.

Matthew 9: 27-31

"Then he touched their eyes and said, according to your faith will it be done to you (Matthew 9:29)."

THE PEOPLE'S life is restoring the essence of life. In Hebrews 11:1, 2, talk about the fundamental nature of life. It is said that faith that trusts God entirely is a solid foundation that makes life most worthwhile.

The fundamental fact of life is this. This belief in God is a solid foundation that makes life worthwhile. Faith is a clue that allows you to see what you can not see.

There is nothing as difficult as having faith in life. But if you want to get faith, it is faith that you get easily. Those who are not interested in eternal life, those who are not even interested in putting their feet on the world of faith, it is very powerful to have faith. However, with an interest in faith and active listening to the Word, the seed of faith will easily grow into the field of mind.

The Lord speaks. If you want to have faith first, you have to hope and believe in what you can not hope for. We need a more positive attitude toward faith that wants to see and hear, even if it is not audible. Even if you are not interested in the spiritual world, there is an opportunity for everyone to gain faith. To qualify as a Christian and to live as a people of this land, you must be qualified. That is, the eyes of faith must be opened.

He said that faith is hope and believing in hope. It is true belief that you can see and hear what you have not seen before then what you have already seen and heard. The Lord speaks of our attitude toward faith through the text. As Jesus walked down the street, there were people who followed him.

WHY DID THEY FOLLOW HIM? AND WHAT ARE THEIR WISHES?

Jesus healed Jairus' daughter and a woman who had suffered from blood diseases for 12 years. And this healing rumor spread throughout the land. Good rumors also give hope to the listener but bad rumors that are not good cause despair and discouragement. And let them be captivated by fear. Christians must listen to rumors and discern. There are rumors of killing people's souls and rumors of saving them. The rumors of Jesus' healing were rumors of saving people. And this rumor is heard by two blind people. You will save the dead and you will hear that the Lord has healed them for 12 years. The blind knew that their illness was a disease that man could not fix.

It was an incurable illness that no one could see. Now, there are many kinds of medicine that develop the technique, make the eyes open and brighten the eyes, but there was nothing at that time. If you do not see the front, you will have to live your whole life like that. It was the illness that afflicts them as much as blood disease for them. The blind man has been following the Lord with confidence that he has the healing power. This is the attitude of obtaining the first faith we should learn.

Faith must have something to follow with hope. It was an important life decision for the blind that made him decide to follow the Lord. Faith has the ability to lead people. He who does not have faith has no hope and does not follow. There must be an act of interest and follow-up to Jesus. There are those who want Jesus to follow. They have to be passive and think that the Lord must be active.

Of course, the Lord is also a discerning and weary visitor, but it is important that we seek the Lord first.

It is important that we are resurrected and that the Lord visits the disciples on the shore of Galilee, but we also need to have faith to visit the resurrected Lord. The blind man followed rumors of truth. They just followed it. When they followed him, they believed that the Lord would look after them and be merciful. The blind follow the Lord with a prayerful title. It is asking them to have pity on themselves. They wanted to have mercy on once and look round about. There was no need for them as much as this. It was his only desire to look around and pay attention to them. Jesus did not respond immediately to their cry. The situation now is on the road. This is in contrast to the 12-year bloody woman. The disease of the woman was fixed on the spot. But when the blind men cried out to the Lord, the Lord did not answer in that place, and once he entered the house. Why did he go home?

It was just to see the reaction of the blind. If there is no answer even if you cry, give up easily and go back and it is over. Before Jesus answered, they saw that they were waiting and followed.

Jesus went into a house. Yet the blind do not give up but follow the Lord even to the house. And they come before the Lord and ask for mercy on them.

WHAT DID JESUS SAY TO THE BLIND AT HOME? WHY DID HE SAY THIS?

The Lord saw that they had a faith to be healed. But this is not enough. Once again their conviction was needed. Jesus asked them, "Do you believe that I can do this?" Do you really believe that I can do this? They were enough to have a faith worthy of healing, not only that they followed the home without giving up, and that they should have mercy on them. But on the Lord's side, it is also lacking. Their will is important, but above all, faith in the Lord is more important.

So Jesus asked if he had confidence in the Son of God as the one who could heal. Jesus said through the text what true faith is. True faith is what we hope and believe in a situation we can not hope for. Now their eyes are wrapped, but if they were the Lord, they believed that they would open their wounded eyes.

Though the eyes are wrapped around, their eyes have already left their eyes. What should be preceded by miracles in the flesh are the miracles that occur in the mind. You will be discouraged from the heart and no miracle will arise. If you think of it, there will be no change. The Lord has healed the cripples of the heart before the physical deeds. The blind are the Lord in the words of the Lord. They believe that the Lord will heal them.

After hearing the words, the Lord touches his eyes and says, "Let it be your faith." He did not ask for seeing. He just told me to be faithful. What does this mean? As much as your faith, it will work. It means. It is as much as I believe. It also applies to us. We are as faithful as we are. The Lord asks us for faith. It is so important that we live and have faith. It is much more beneficial to us to have than to not have faith.

It is so good to have faith that people bear the burden of having faith. When we have faith, there are many things that are much more helpful to us. What we need to get first in the world is not wealth or honor. First of all, we need to get faith. The blind chose the best. And as the blind believed, their eyes were brightened.

WHAT DID THE LORD CALL UPON THEM AFTER THEIR EYES WERE OPENED?

Jesus told them not to tell anyone about the history of the miracle. Why? This is to prevent misunderstandings of people.
If the miraculous signs of Jesus were to become known, it would be clear that the Jews would hold up Jesus as a fleshly disease and a political messiah to save them from Roman oppression. This is quite different from the intention of Jesus on earth. There was a risk that the original purpose would be altered. If so, the meaning of Jesus' crucifixion of salvation is faded and may be disturbed by people, so the Lord has told us not to. We must know precisely about Jesus Christ.

We continue to study the ministry of Jesus' power. Most of them are focused on the ministry of healing and ministry of the miracle. One thing to keep in mind is that all these ministries can never be ahead of Jesus' cross the ministry. The most important ministry of Jesus is the ministry of salvation. It is the faith of resurrection. You must always remember the original meaning of the Lord's coming. Even if you believe in the Lord, you must know and trust what the Lord is. But people are interested in something else. It is important not to focus on solving their problems but to believe in the Lord.

{Meditation Point}
1)Faith is a holy act that follows the Lord. It is a heart that desires to find the Lord. Do we have such a heart and a passion?
2)What do you consider Him in your life? How deep is his involvement in my life?

CHAPTER 17

MOUTH IS OPEN.

Matthew 9: 32-34

"And when the demon was driven out, the man who had been mute spoke. The crowd was amazed and said, Nothing like this has ever seen in Israel (Matthew 9:33)."

THE WORDS from the body (flesh) which is raised by the sin are always negative. If you do not live in the Spirit, the thoughts of the body become dominant. This idea is not progressive. "I can not do that." "How can a person like me do this?" "I can never do that." If you get caught up in these negative thoughts, you'll be a loser.

Let us rely on the words of the Spirit rather than the flesh. There are positive words, "I can do it," and "I'll start again." The negative person does not have a vital language to speak. The word itself is dead, and the dead language is used in combination.

People are not the ones who are caught in negative words. The people have a vision. They have a dream. There is a great plan given by the Lord. The word 'people' in the past made their language by shouting hope in the shadows of society. People's words move society and transform the times. John the Baptist calls himself a cry out in the wilderness. What is the cry?

It is a voice that awakens the spiritually sleeping people to prepare the way of the Lord. His words are not words of killing people, but truths that lead to the right way. The word of truth is the language of life that can reach the people most. The wicked do not speak of life. Those who are good in heart, those who are clean, and those who are hungry for righteousness, produce words of life. "A good man brings goodness out of the good stored up in his heart, and an evil man brings evil things out of the evil stored up in his heart. For out of the outflow of his heart his mouth speaks" (Luke 6:45). "Out of the same mouth come praise, and cursing, my brother, this should not be" (James 3:10). In the Bible, many words are spoken, and most of the words associated with them are Proverbs and Ecclesiastes. "Even if the mouth of the righteous is the fountain of life ..., and the lips of the discerning have wisdom,"

As soon as a person is born, he begins to learn to speak. Personality is created by learning words. It becomes a person. Words play a very important role in growth. Failure to speak is like being unable to grow.

As children begin to learn to speak, their mind grows, and all the things they need to live and do are started at the same time. The Bible says that good and evil coexist in our words. A good word, an evil word, is in the heart together and comes out through words. The wicked usually bring out evil words from their minds. But a good man picks out good words in good minds. According to what is in our hearts, the word of the person will be revealed.

Some of the ministries of Jesus' healing ministry were to open speech. Not only did he open the speech of man, but he healed even the things contained in his heart.

A DEMON-POSSESSED MAN

When people bring a person who can not speak to the Lord, He opens the eyes of the blind. It is spiritually and physically blind that he can not see. But the Lord opened his eyes to faith and made him see the Lord. And he made him live a new life. Think that you can not talk because you can not see the eyes and it is frustrating. How frustrating? If you stay without speaking for a day, you will feel that you want to talk in your mind and accumulate things like wanting to express more. Then, when you have a chance to say, you start to pour everything in front of people that you have pressed so far. This is a very important life to talk. When he can not speak and express his own will, he chooses the extreme way.

HOW DID THE LORD HEAL A MAN WHO COULD NOT SPEAK? WHO IS THE LORD?

As soon as a demon-possessed man came to Jesus, he knew that the demon was, and he was driven out. When the demon went out, he was freed from all that was holding him. It is because the mind is released and the speech is over.

He wonders what the first word he spoke as the speech began to burst. He is not listed in the Word, but he must have been pleased and liked. When you speak properly, you will enjoy the joy of solving and solving everything in your mind. The Lord has freed us. We must know the identity of the demon.

In the text, this man says that the demon has been heard. There are several reasons. There is also a congenital or acquired cause. And there is a spiritual reason. It is possible to know to some extent what the demon is doing. The demon is a hindrance to the right speech. It blocks the words of justice. It blocks the words of love. It is making the confession of faith impossible. This man was pressed against the power of demons for a lifetime. Jesus took what he could not speak seriously.

Confession of faith is indeed important. Jesus healed and made conversation with the patients. And he asked if he was willing to be healed. A great work arose in those who believe, and those who confess but this man could not speak, so he could not tell whether he had such a doctor or not. So Jesus saw the heart of the man who was blocked and healed him. Jesus means to know our hearts well. Jesus, who observes my spirit even though I can not speak, is the one who sees and works in our hearts. As you know the circumstances of those who can not speak, the Lord wants to understand and be with us in the midst of untold pain and afflictions.

No one liked to speak as much as Jesus. Even though he spoke, he understood the mind of the person well and understood the word of the audience. It was quite different from the teaching of the Pharisees who were at the scene said that this was not the case among Israel, and they envied even the most popular Jesus. One of the reasons Jesus did well was because he had read more than anyone. It is because we know our circumstances. He is the Lord who wants to talk with us.

"I waited patiently for the LORD; he turned to me and heard my cry. He lifted me out of the slimy pit, out of the mud and mire; he set my feet on a rock and gave me a firm place to stand. He put a new song in my mouth, a hymn of praise to our God. Many will see and fear and

put their trust in the Lord. (Psalm 40: 1)"
"I proclaim righteousness in the great assembly; I do not seal my
lips, as you know, O LORD. (40: 9)"

The Lord knew that there was power in words. By knowing he knew that blessings and curses also came. So he always taught his disciples to confess their faith. He told me to build up good things in my heart so that I could control my mind well and get lots of good words. The disciples are ahead of a great ministry.

He first gave them the Holy Spirit to cleanse all the evil things and fill them with the Word filled with faith and love. For the disciples, were all those who needed the help of the Lord. We should go to them and comfort them with good words. It was because the role of the disciples was important in order for the truth to stand.

We must not forget that the Lord is the one who opens our speech.

He wants us to be victorious Christians by opening our spiritually blocked mouth and believing in the Lord.

{Meditation Point}

1)Is not there anything I can not speak?
2)I must leave for my heart to the Holy Father. The Holy Spirit must come and fill with the things that the Lord is pleased that the speech of faith will be opened.

CHAPTER 18

THE SMALLEST THING IS IN THE EYES OF FAITH

John 6: 1-14

"Jesus them took the loves, gave thanks, and distributed to those who were seated as much as they wanted. He did the same with the fish (John 6:11)."

- Knowing gives faith and not knowing fear. - The writing on the wall of a driving school

THERE IS a big difference between knowing and not knowing like this. You need to know more than you do not know. The people are enlightened. The people are not ignorant. They have advanced the age of change and reform by learning the truth by knowing. The Lord has come to earth to enlighten the unbelievers in the spiritual world and to make known the truth.

He enjoyed teaching them every time he met people. It is so important to know. If you know anything about, even if you know something a little bit confident and difficult, you will cope wisely. Problems arise when you do not know. If you know a little bit about a car, you know how to drive. Like if you do not know how to drive, you get scared. Our faith is becoming more and more enriched as we learn more and more. Faith is the mystery of faith that true faith is not the ability to make our lives poverty but the ability to live to enrich and sharing together.

WHERE DID JESUS GO, AND WHO FOLLOWED HIM? WHAT PURPOSE DID THEY FOLLOW?

He wanted to go across the sea to Tiberias. Then there were those who followed Jesus. It was not a small group but a large group. They all wanted to hear Jesus' words and were willing to fulfill their spiritual thirst. They were those who needed help. The Bible also clearly explains why they follow.

They saw the signs that he did to the sick. The crowds followed Jesus because their circumstances were desperate. It was an age of spiritual hunger. It was the age when many fruits were waiting for the harvest. They are already fruitful waiting for the harvest. Someone should go and tell Jesus' love and lead him to the Lord. Jesus did not rebuke the followers who followed him. He wanted to help them at any rate. The Passover, the Jewish holiday, was near the time. Even though it was a holiday, it was long since people's joy was gone. A holiday is a day of joy and a day with family, but their present situation is not at all. They were not happy, they were being chased, and they had only a sincere heart. Jesus looked up to them. The expression of having listened to eyes means that he showed interest in the Bible. "Who can show us any good? Let the light of your face shine upon us, O Lord, (Psalm 4: 6)."

If we shine the Lord's face on us once, we will be raised again. It is a happier life to live with the attention of God than to live with the attention of people. People's attention is temporary. It is not forever. People's attention is always changing around. But the Lord's concern is not. The Lord's concern for us is eternal. Jesus also began to pay attention to the crowd. And he sees the problem with them. The followers of the Lord knew that they were hungry for lack of food. Eating is the most basic problem. Jesus tells Philip, "Where can you buy bread and feed these people?" It is not a negative word. Jesus was already convinced that he could feed them and asked for the attitude of his disciples.

Jesus' heart is like a man, and his disciples wanted to have a belief that even though there are many, God can feed them. So this is a question already answered. Still, Philip makes an unanswered answer to the question. Even if you give it a little, you must have the money of two hundred denarii(Eight months' wages). Philip tried to answer faithfully. He calculated the amount and told the Lord how much money it would cost. Philip's words are not wrong. It's really amazing computing power. The children and adults are all about 20,000 people, and they are kind enough to say that they will have tens of thousands of won for sharing. But this answer is an answer that excludes the Lord from thought. If the Lord is not there, of course, such big money goes into it. The limits of Philip are revealed here.

Philip is what we are. He is a person who pointed to Philip and turned his eyes to reality. I have come to the conclusion that I can not do what I can and can not do in reality, and that I can not do it in advance. We also think about what I can do and fear beforehand, and then I worry about what to do next. It means that there are many people like Philip around.

WHO IS SPEAKING TO HIM WITH FAITH? WHAT DID HE DO?

As soon as Philip's words are over, Andrew goes. Andrew was listening to all of Philip's conversation with the Lord. Andre was the same disciple but had a different view from Philip.

There was another idea. Even though he was a member of Jesus, all these thoughts were different. The vision they had in mind was different. Andrew's thoughts can be considered more unrealistic than Philip thought. Andrew does not count like Philip, but just five barley loaves and two fish. How do you do this with so many people? He says. This is not a negative word, but it is like saying, "Let the Lord give you an offer, and let the Lord do it with this once."

Jesus, unlike Philip, was pleased with Andrew's offer. If this is the Lord's power, we can feed the crowds anyway. It is like saying. The Lord began to let every man sit down at the end of Andrew's saying on the lawn. First, the Lord congratulated the five loaves and two fish. He thanked firstly. It was a small rice cake and a fish, but it was given to God first. And after he was thankful, he began to give it to the crowd. However, the fish and bread started to come out continuously from the basket. There was a history that filled the twelve baskets without throwing away all the sculptures that came out enough to eat enough for them.

The Lord first blessed God before feeding the crowds. He thanked God. Although it is a small amount, it was first given to God. We also need an attitude first to God. No matter how small, we must have a mind to think of God first. The attitude of giving is not something that I used first and then eat. It is the first thing to distinguish.

This is the basic attitude. It is like waiting for the son to eat the spoon and to take the food first in the table. It means not to fill your stomach first but to wait for God to give thanks. I hope that I will not give you what you spend, but you will be a saint to God first.

WHAT IS THE REALIZATION THAT THIS INCIDENT GIVES US?

Pity

We must have a heart of compassion for the person. The disciples and Jesus were different in their view of the multitudes. The disciples had the idea that if they were hungry, they would solve it. But Jesus wanted to feed the multitudes themselves. It was not easy to chase the people who came to hear the words of Jesus. When you feel compassion for people, you will find ways to feed them.

You must have a sense of the problem.

Second, we must actively seek solutions with a sense of the problem. Do not be silent and find what you can do best.
Philip was just counting, and Andrew found a clue that could solve the problem among the crowd. If you find the path ahead actively, you will see a way.

The smallest thing is the eyes of faith.

The third is to see with the eyes of faith. No matter how small and insignificant it is, if it is caught in the hands of God's power, there is no work that can not be accomplished. But in Andrew's eyes, he had the assurance that what would happen if this small, insignificant thing entered into the Lord's hands. Even small things made sense.

Always with the possibility in mind

Fourth, He looked at all things with the possibility in mind. He thought that the Lord could do something I could not do and he responded with faith. In the hands of the child, the things were infinite potential in the eyes of the Lord. There was a firm belief that if the Lord were with him, even impossible things could be done.

The principle of richness

Fifth, the five loaves of bread and two fish incident contain the principle of God's abundance. It was a small thing, but when he opened his eyes to the Lord with the eyes of faith, he was given to the Lord, and there was a work that left many people eating and full of twelve baskets. The Lord guides our lives and does not lead them to poverty. It is always someone who is able to fulfill the history that is full of things and overflowing and to share with others as much as it is.

{Meditation Point}

1)Do not I have a face like Philip?
2)Let's think about the Lord you have given before sharing the five loaves of bread.
3)What are my five loaves of bread and two fish to present before the Lord?

CHAPTER 19

FAITH IN FOCUS

Matthew 14: 22-33

"Immediately Jesus reached out his hand and caught him. You of little faith, He said, why did you doubt? (Matthew 14:31)"

AN ATHLETE who has lost concentration can not expect good results in the field. People who have experience with burning paper with a convex lens during childhood will know better. If you do not collect the sunlight in one place, the paper will not burn. When light is concentrated in one place, the paper will catch fire. The sickle must be changed frequently for the grass to be well cut.

A lazy farmer does not spend time grooming an extension. However, the farmer who prepares always cares for the extension of labor for more efficient labor. Anything is a difference in concentration.

In order to make a lot of effect with a small investment, it is necessary to train to concentrate in our life. Then what about faith? The Lord often used concentration to proclaim the truth.

Numerous people came to the mountain to hear the word. Talking to people rather than talking to one distracts attention and reduces concentration. But to the Lord, this was an exception. The Lord proclaimed the Word with a concentration in front of tens of thousands of crowds. Many crowds were concentrated in the Lord and heard the Word. Not only that. When he raised the miracle, he approached the object and showed the concentration of faith and only to focus on looking at Him alone.

The world is full of things to dissipate our attention. What does the Bible say?

It is that there are so many scattered around things that disturb the life of faith, such as the world's wealth and concern (anxiety), pride, and lust of the eye. There is a wide range of things to watch and listen to because it is so wide for those who walk on broad streets. Going to see here and there, the goal that you want in your mind will also become blurred. But those who walk on narrow streets are not. Pay attention to narrow terrain. Will it fall? Be careful and take steps one by one. He who walks a narrow path is not a fool but a wise man; he is the wisest of those who acquire great things after investing small things.

WHERE DID JESUS WALK AT DAWN? AND WHAT WAS THE RESPONSE OF THE DISCIPLES?

The disciples were stooping forward. But before them, a storm is waiting. The life of faith is moving forward. It is not retreating backward. A lot of difficulties wait in front.

He promised to give the land of Canaan, but before that, he had accumulated such problems as the Jordan, Jericho, and Ai. We must overcome this and move forward. The enemies are always waiting.

The Lord leads us sometimes to a restful abundant waterfront, but sometimes to a place like the valley of Aghal, like the wilderness. The disciples are fishermen and experts in the sea. The storm can come to them too. No matter how faithful people are, the test is always waiting.

The problem is our attitude when a dangerous situation comes. Jesus goes everywhere. Now, when he saw the disciples in trouble, they did not know it. He visited them. The time is between 4 am and 6 am at night. In time, the disciples were at least nine hours fighting the storm. John 6:19 says that he went ten times.

It would be 4-5 kilometers for nine hours. The Lord has come to them in times of crisis when they may die. And he walked on the water, saying, "Do not be afraid." What does this mean? Do not worry. Your hardships are now over. There is no worry because the Lord is with us.

The Lord came to comfort the disciples undergoing hardship. We have a time of rowing in the storm of life. There is a time when I feel like I am alone in the world of nobody who can help me.

But the important thing is that Jesus is always looking for me. When they meet difficulties, they all run away. The love, the family, the company, and all the people I know leave me, but the Lord does not leave and comes to me.

WHAT KIND OF PERSON DID JESUS WALK ON THE WATER, AND WHAT DID THE DISCIPLES DO IN FRONT OF THE LORD?

Jesus did not walk along the beach. At that time of the dawn, there is a view that anyone can distinguish where he is. Jesus did not walk on the beach but walked in the middle of the sea far from the land.

It is already mentioned in the Word. Jesus, walking on the water, did not see the water under his feet. This was not an obstacle for Jesus. Jesus is a perfect man and at the same time living God. Jesus was also in a frail body. Now, Jesus walked on the water by concentrating only on God with dependence on God. Through the faith of Jesus walking on the water like this, we are well aware of what kind of faith attitude we should have in this world where troublesome and rough winds are always waiting. The Lord, who came by walking on the water, first calmed the storm. But Peter says, "If the Lord calls, command me to walk on the water." The Lord permitted it.

At first Peter walked a few steps as he watched the Lord, and suddenly he was terrified by the waves of his feet. He saw the wind. A moment of change of mind occurred. This is why he began worrying about whether he would fall into the water. Because faith is lost and the Lord is lost in sight, the real problem has come. As soon as he thinks of this, he falls into the water.

The Lord escapes Peter, who is lost and drowsy. And he said. "You have a little faith, why do you doubt?"

Peter first saw Jesus larger than the waves. I will be safe because Jesus is with us. I had the idea. However, since I am stepping on the wave right now, the problem of reality is approaching. I saw the waves louder than Jesus. I have lost sight of the Lord. Peter used the word "if". "If you give it," This word has many meanings. Peter wondered about who came to the water now. I wanted to know who is making this impossible. Things that were impossible among people could not be easily seen.

So Peter doubted his eyes. Peter thought that this great thing could not be done without the Lord. So Peter wanted to make sure that his doubts were on his knees. It is possible because it is the Lord rather than the word. Peter needed a certain conviction. In our faith, the word 'if' should be omitted. 'If', the word is like a transaction. It is a word looking at the price. If you are Lord, please let me walk. Then I will acknowledge you as Lord. It means to do business with the Lord.

It is not "I will devote myself to the Lord if it does." If you become rich, we will build an orphanage. If the stock goes up, I will donate. It is not good attitudes. The Lord does not want to bargain with us. What the Lord wants is faith to concentrate. It is not the faith, but the Lord. It is the faith. We have no choice but to hang on to the Lord. He is the Lord who will deliver us. Therefore, you should focus on this Lord while living so that you do not miss Him in the sight of my life.

We must focus on the Lord who matures our faith through suffering. Our faith life is the faith to focus on Jesus.

Hebrews 12: 2 says, "Let us fix our eyes on Jesus, the author, and perfector of our faith, who for the joy set before him endured the cross, scorning its shame, and sat down at the right hand of the throne of God". Faith fails when you focus on yourself. If you focus on the environment, you fall. If you focus on people, you have to be disappointed. We should focus only on Jesus.

The Israelites complained that the way was bad and focused on the environment. And they soon sinned.

God will send a bronze serpent on the pole to them who are dying. (Nu 21: 8). He said. The pole symbolizes the cross. In John's Gospel, he speaks of Jesus. He who dies in the midst of sin will live by looking at Jesus. What I look for is to look closely. If you do not have any other thoughts and focus on the Lord, you will have a clear path ahead of us. If the problem is complex, the more complicated the problem, the simpler and principled solution can be solved. The cross is a simple truth. Just look at it. The more complex the complexity, the more you will have to give your eyes to Jesus. Faith is not self-confidence. It is not philosophy either. Trusting and following completely.

Our Jesus is the one who keeps the storm of suffering silent. And through all these processes, we are able to further mature our faith. The world is full of things to take our eyes off. The darker they appear, the more clearly they appear. Let me see the environment and see my situation. And it makes me think differently.

{Meditation Point}

In the church, we need an attitude that focuses on the Lord. It is not in front of a man to serve and dedicate but to do before God.

1)Have you ever been in a situation where we are alone in the wilderness? Who should we wait for?
2)Have you ever missed your sight in our faith life? Are you living your life in all aspects of the Lord?

CHAPTER 20

YOU HAVE SPOKEN LIKE THIS,

Mark 7: 24-30

"Then he told her, for such a reply, you may go; the demon has left your daughter (Mark 7:29)."

WHAT DOES speech mean to us? Some scholars say that the speech is the character of the person, the culture. Through the word, the entire person is revealed. Nothing is hidden from the word. Our mind is a container of words.

A word cleanses a person's mind and gives salvation, but it also gives the worst thing through words. Our tongue has both sides. Evil words come out and good words come out according to what the mind controls. There was one thing in common in the lives of the greatest men in history.

In any environment, he was able to speak well. They did not say anything negative. Even though the situation was always worse, the words from the mouth were positive words. Speaking a lot is not a wise person. The most necessary and appropriate words play an excellent role.

Winston Churchill has risen up Britain, falling through the shortest and most convincing rhetoric of we will never give up in the podium to the desperate British people. A word that is more powerful than ten million words is the most valuable and precious.

The people who live on this land should be people who rule well. The people whom the Lord loves and wants are more positive than negative words and accidents, and they wanted to live with the words of faith. He wanted to change the way people live. So the Lord loved those who said good words, faith words. Whatever he is, the words of faith have become the power to move the Lord's heart. Today we want to know the heart of the Lord. He wants to pray and know what his will is. The way to know is simple. It is a word of faith and a positive word in my mouth. That is the will of the Lord.

WHERE DID JESUS GO? AND WHERE DID HE GO FROM THERE?

Jesus left the place called Capernaum and went to the provinces of Tire and Sidon. He did many ministries in Capernaum and moved his ministry to a new place. He did not stay in one place. As he witnessed the Gospel, he went to many areas and met many people. This area is called the Syrian Phoenicia area. Near the Mediterranean Sea, many people were living in fishing and commerce.

Wherever there is a person and where there is a need for help, Jesus has visited and has met. There he entered a house. He tried to come in quietly to pray, but he could not hide it. People have come to the house of the Lord how they heard the rumor that He came. Who is the Lord? In short, he is a good person. He is good and full of mercy. If you are a good person, people want to meet you once. I do not want to meet an evil person, a person who gives harm to me. Because Jesus is a good person, people are trying to meet each other.

Why is he good? He listens to our prayers and gives us blessings. He is someone who understands our circumstances better than anyone else. Therefore, those who seek this Lord are blessed. There is no distinction in seeking the Lord. It is not what a particular person is looking for. The Lord is good. Anyone who thinks that you are the Lord enough to be the master of my life can find you.

Today's text shows that everyone in the world can find the Lord. It tells us through the text that the Lord does not discriminate by what he has, and is not discriminated by what he has learned.

WHO CAME TO YOU? WHAT WAS YOUR HEART TOWARD HER?

A woman came. The woman was a Canaanite woman, and by chance, she was a Greek. The Bible does not tell the name. It just comes out as a provincial born (Syrian Phoenicia). It is easy to use the name of the province. The presence of this woman did not give any meaning to the Jews because it is a stranger. If the name is not mentioned in the Bible, it is often ignored, and the name is not mentioned when it is passed by. Perhaps the Jews would have thought of this woman as a trivial entity but no matter how strangers, the problem was the same. Her problem was her child's problem. The child is a great title of prayer in her life.

Her child was haunted. And she was not a grown-up adult but a young daughter. The young daughter hugs love in the house. She is a lovely child.

However, the precious daughter is hurting her parents because she is haunted by evil spirits. If you look at your child from the perspective of your parents, you are sick and upset. It was the parents' mind that they wanted to be sick instead of their daughter if at all possible. She was looking for the Lord because she could not stand still because of the poor mood toward her child. She came to know that He was a good man. She is only asking to get rid of the demons without falling down at the feet of the Lord. This woman is praying to the Lord. The Gentiles are praying to the Lord. What is the Lord's response? But in fact, the Lord's intentions were quite different.

From the beginning, the Lord had pity on this woman. The Lord always observed the reaction and attitude of the other side in ministry. Does she have a place to be saved? You have seen faith. Most ministries have always been linked to faith.

Those who have faith have been healed and saved, and history has arisen without distinction between Gentiles and Jews. The Lord is now rejecting the woman without permission, disappointed. "Tell your children to eat first, and not to take your child's bread and throw it to the dogs."

This means that if you correctly interpret the Bible, "you are a dog." The Jews are children of God, and you are a dog that should not be equal. How insulting is it? It means that self-esteem goes bad. If you are a normal person, your self-esteem would be so bad that your mind would have turned away. Unlike even rumors, Jesus might have thought he was not a good person.

Faith is beyond the limit. If we can not justify our self-esteem and acknowledge the words of Jesus, the work of faith can never happen. This is what Jesus demands of the woman. Even a Gentile has demanded such a faith to acknowledge God. She has lived like a stranger like a dog until now, but in order to settle her past life and live as a new child, she had to put all of her things behind and look at the Lord.

Surprisingly, however, this woman had such a belief. "Lord, if you are right, the dogs under the table eat the crumbs the children eat." It was a stranger, but it is a wise word indeed. She wasn't angry at what the Lord had said, and did not rebel, "I am a sinner!" She accepted the word of the Lord and acknowledged herself. This is like the confession of Peter. "Yes, that's right. I am a sinner. But even though sinners have lived a doglike life, do dogs not eat crumbs from their masters? It is. I confess that my daughter can be clean if I can impart to Him at least a little bit of grace like that crumbs."

We hate to admit ourselves. If I ask you to acknowledge and help me in the sight of the Lord, you will receive me as I am, and you will be with me. You will not accept Him because you do not acknowledge Him, and your relationship with Him will become increasingly distant. You should not be arrogant. Pride is the enemy that breaks spiritual fellowship with God.

We must lower ourselves to the Lord and long for the Lord's help. Jesus, by the word, knew that the woman was a modest woman, and said to her: "I have said this". What does this mean? I am a dog, and I am filled with a woman's willingness to accept the same grace as the crumbs of the Lord. The words of the woman impressed the heart of the Lord.

It has moved the heart of the Lord. The word represents the state of mind of the person. No matter how you try to conceal your heart, conversation is one of the things that are hidden in your mind. For Christians, speaking is important. History speaks a word. The person's personality is revealed in a word. There are many meanings in the words of the pagan woman. The spirit of a young daughter who is suffering from demons in a single word of a simple answer, such as a heart that lowers herself and raises the Lord, a desperate desire, a love for a child, a persistent faith that does not give up, As she returned home, her daughter who was already lying on the bed had improved. We also want to be a recognized saint before the Lord "because we have said this."

There was a man named Bob Wieland. He was a marathon runner. But there are no two legs. He stepped on a land mine in the Vietnam War and lost both legs. However, Bob Wieland completed a 42.195-kilometer full course in just two hands at the Los Angeles Marathon. The others are two or three hours away, and Wieland crawls and finishes for a week. In 1982, he crawled 4454 kilometers of North

American continent with two arms and two spirals. He completed it in 3 years, 8 months and 6 days. A lot of people were impressed by his actions and joined together, but the normal people gave up when they crossed the New Mexico desert over 60 degrees Celsius and left without leaving one. At this time, he will confess. "All the people have left me, but only God has kept me by my side." He thought that he had two hands without giving up when he lost both feet. He said he was always saying that he could do whatever he wanted.

{Meditation Point}

1) Do you think that He is a savior who can save me from all kinds of situations?
2) What words are on my lips and how can I confess before the Lord?

CHAPTER 21

OPENING HISTORY

Mark 7: 31-37

"He looked up to heaven and with a deep sigh said to hem, *Ephphatha*! (Which means, *be opened!*) (Mark 7:34)."

EVERYONE HAS flaws in man. Where is the man living without fault? The greatest enemy of life is not in the outside, but in us. Man does not blame the enemy inside. It is the original mind of a person to pass responsibility. It was Satan who tempted Eve, but it was Eve who eventually fell into temptation. Before that, God had already given the law to humans in the Garden of Eden.
The first law was perfect. God established the most perfect law in the Garden. What is the fundamental meaning of the law? It is the very thing that sets human beings right before God. It is the law that is the same as the one who makes the right path without departing from the will of God.

God has told us not to eat fruit in the garden. At the moment of breaking the law, humans invade the realm of God, and the boundary between the Creator and the creature is destroyed. Eve is the act of deliberately destroying the commandment of God that gave Eve to the law to not eat. As a result, human beings will see beyond the realm of the Creator and become a descendant of sin. If you can not stop a small gap in the inside, the gap will eventually grow bigger, resulting that can not be covered. Everyone has its faults. There is a wrong habit. We live on the shortage and distorted parts. Everyone in the world has always left room for future failures like Eve. How then can you live to fill this gap? We recognize and supplement our own weaknesses. We are defective at present.

The moment that acknowledges its imperfection, it can be rather easily buried. When we recognize ourselves as a sinful being, we have room for salvation. When you are open to in yourself, you will see what you do not have from that moment and your eyes will turn on the path of new truth. The people should be able to look back on their inner side. The eyes must be opened to realize that he is present and to acknowledge that he himself is never a complete person. People are those who need help. When their closed life is opened, when they find a true figure, they know that the Lord is there.

Who brought the one who was deaf and stumbled in the text to the Lord? Let's think about the person who came without the help of the person alone.

The one who was deaf and stumbled did not come to Jesus alone. He came to Jesus with the help of people. He who was deaf and stuttered was not able to hear and speak well, but he was able to see and walk by himself. He is the one who can come to him alone. There are two reasons why.

HIS APPEARANCE WAS POOR.

First, because his appearance was poor it was embarrassing that he could not hear and speak well. He can not speak well to others. If someone else was speaking, it would have been impossible for them to just hear it.

It is failure to speak at the time means that the pronunciation is inaccurate and inability to express his/her intention properly. People who stutter are often said to lack self-confidence. There are a myriad of words to say in your mind, but you can not tell your opinion if you are only in front of you. It is heartfelt, but the words that come out of your mouth are confident, shameful, and especially unheard-of. Words only go into thought, but the words that come out of the mouth are very limited. This person is well aware of his faults. He knows so much about his inferiority that he could not hear or speak well. But he was hesitant because he doesn't have a confidence.

HE DID NOT HEAR IT AT ALL.

The second is that he has not heard at all. Jesus has done so many ministries. As he moved the provinces, he made a history of grace. People preached the rumor about this Jesus from mouth to mouth. There are a lot of rumors about Jesus in all over the country. However, he can not listen to this person, so if someone does not explain it, he will not know what Jesus is if he does not care. How is faith built? It is built from listening. Faith is due to hearing. However, it is difficult to have faith because you can not listen to it most basically. People say that even if they go to church, it is difficult to have faith. It is important to know that going to church does not have faith, but that you have to listen carefully to have faith. The reason for going to church is to listen. We are going to hear the word. The most important thing to come to the church is to listen to the word of God and keep it. This poor man could not hear nor speak, so it was difficult to have faith.

We do not know how many of these people are around us. There are still many people who can not live a life of faith because there is no one to tell the truth. What we have to do for these people is to take their hands and lead them to Jesus. In the text, people brought the hand of a man who could not hear, and brought him to Jesus and asked him to do so. He said, "I beg you to lay hands on me."

I begged you to take care of myself right away. Ordination means putting your hands up. It means. If you are asking for an ordination, the people who brought the sickness should be considered to have some degree of faith, because he knew the ability of ordination. Ordination is not done by anyone, has spiritual authority. Most of all, the person who is ordained or who is ordained must absolutely trust and assure the power of God. Jesus did the laying on of hands, praying always to God and having the authority of the Son of God and laying hands on him.

The person who receives the ordination must also not doubt that he is the Lord. If you are ordained, you must have confidence that you will be faithful. In doing so, the ministry of the power comes through the laying on of hands. Ordinance can bring comfort, heal the wounds of the mind, leave the disease, and solve the problem. Ordination is an interest. Putting his hand on his head means that God is compassionate and caring for him. Jesus also loved to lay hands on them. When I prayed for the sick and prayed for my children, I put my hands and prayed. Jesus showed interest and love.

HOW DID JESUS GO TO THOSE WHO DEMANDED ORDINATION? AND WHAT DID HE SAY TO HIM? LET'S THINK ABOUT THE REASON HE SPOKE.

Jesus raised his hands, not putting his hands on his head, but putting his fingers in his ears, spitting and touching his tongue. The fact that he put his fingers in ears and spit hands and touched tongue should be seen as a more aggressive response to the demands of people's laying on hands. Although people only asked to be ordained, Jesus did a more real and definite ordination than their petition. He will take his hand directly to the lesion. We should look at the problem of what this person has now by treating the affected person correctly. Jesus is the one who can heal with his spit, put his fingers in his ears, and heal without putting his hands on his head. But this patient was unheard and unable to speak, and the people who brought them asked for the laying on of hands.

However, Jesus kindly wanted to show his intention to act by his actions rather than words. Putting his fingers in ears has shown them that you are healing ears now, and you have shown before your hands that you are healing your tongue now that you can not speak. According to the condition of the patient, Jesus devoted himself. It is the person who resolves the problem carefully while it looks like a caring doctor. Jesus knows exactly what our problems are. He knows what my current spiritual condition is. Because Jesus knows all of my things, he draws out and heals problems from within me, specifically one by one exactly. We experience a lot of prayer experience. There are many problems. There are many times when it is frustrating where to solve it. But when you receive answers to prayer, there are times when you experience problems that are solved one by one. Why? God knows our affairs well. And one by one, the problem is solved by removing it.

Jesus now touches his body and speaks. *"Ephphatha! Open it!"* Ephphatha will open soon. It means that the ears and speech are open. The ears that have been blocked so far will be pierced and the speech will open. In the words of Jesus, the ears of this man were opened and the miracle of releasing the tongue was raised. Because the tongue that was formed was released, the words sound clear and clear. He can hear his voice clearly what he is saying now.

It has escaped all the problems that have caused him to feel inferior. The things that have always confounded before the people with this matter have caused the Lord to be released. It is a miracle that the wounds and hurting that have been touched by the heart has been healed by the Lord's hands and the words that have been made in the heart. Anyone who comes to the Lord will open a closed problem, open the way, and release the things that have been settled. I hope that the history of *Ephphatha* can come before us.

{Meditation Point}

1)What is my inferiority? Have you ever experienced a lot of history through ordination?
2)How has He led me so far? Do you believe that the Lord who touches and heals even a small part of my life is still the Lord of the power to open the way of many problems before me and to unlock all that I have made?

CHAPTER 22

LET'S FEED ON AGAIN.

Mark 8: 1-9

"The people ate and were satisfied. Afterward the disciples picked up seven basketfuls of broken pieces that were left over (Mark 8:8)."

WHERE IS the happiness of a true life? In Shakespeare's play Henry VI, this dialogue emerges. My crown is not in my head, but in my heart. The decoration of the crown is not diamond. It is invisible jewelry. I am satisfied with this crown by myself. How many kings have used this crown in this world? People are focused only on the splendor that is visible. The people of the world who follow through to the eyes see only true happiness outside. But outside can not find such happiness.

True happiness is in itself. Here is a small ship. This ship should have a sail fitted to its size. If a sail is bigger than a ship, it is easy for the boat to flip over in the wind. If you try to put a large stone in your pocket too small, it will surely be torn into the weight of the stone. In this world we live, people want to have a lot of money. It tries to enjoy higher honor and higher popularity. Of course, not all of these things are bad, but they are always subject to caution. These things make it impossible to know what true happiness is. If you continue to pour water on the brine, the water will lose its salt and lose its true value. There is nothing if you hold a fist; you can catch a lot if you stretch out your hand. He is holding a small thing and losing a big thing. People want to have more. So, what you have now is often dissatisfied. It is our heart to want to move to a greater degree. We can not be happy to get what we want if we want to. What is obtained by seeking leads to greater desire?

If you get away with it, you can deny yourself the desire to have it, and you will be able to live with a feeling of greater satisfaction with what you have. People are always hungry. They are hungry for love and thirst for recognition. There is spiritual hunger. The value of a people is to find oneself and to find true happiness in it.

Our Lord has told us through the Word how we can live and enjoy our lives in our lives.

WHY DID JESUS GIVE THE SAME MIRACLE AS FIVE LOAVES BREAD AND TWO FISH MIRACLE? WHY DID HE REPEAT THE SAME MIRACLE?

In John 10:11, Jesus said, "I am the good shepherd, and the good shepherd shall lay down his life for the sheep." Jesus taught His disciples and the crowd that I am the Good Shepherd. The reason is that Jesus is the one who can feed the hungry sheep. The good shepherd does not see the sheep starving.

In Mongolia there are nomads living in the fields. These are all descendants of Genghis Khan. Most are farmers in the fields. These nomads, however, live in the fields, searching for places where livestock can eat. Where there is a grass, there are hundreds of kilo to thousands of ways, but everywhere that leads to sheep, goats, horses, and cattle and there are good grasses. The good shepherd does not live only for his own benefit, but only to the sheep, only knowing how the sheep can eat. This is Jesus. Jesus wants to feed us. The Lord, the Good Shepherd, wants us to live as the sheep still eat the Word of God and enjoy eternal life. How much interest or love for us is so great that even our lives give our lives for the sheep? We must be Christians who deeply count the hearts of Jesus.

We always try to escape the Lord. There is a lot of curiosity toward the world, and we are going to go out. There is a form that has eternal life, and people will be interested only in other forms. In the wilderness, God offered daily bread. Moses gets complaints from people's mouth because they keep eating. They start to think that they want to have some meat. And they pour out their complaining heart toward Moses. God hears the complaints of the people above. And God sent the quail flock to reproach them for their lack of trust in God. It should not be forgotten that it is our appearance that we are interested in other things and are going to go elsewhere. We must go to Jesus who is our shepherd. When we are in Jesus, eternal food is a guarantee.

WHAT IS THE FUNDAMENTAL REASON FOR JESUS TO PERFORM THE MIRACLE?

He has pity on the weak people who are repeatedly and often falling. Jesus had already fed five thousand people.

Numerous crowds watched miraculous moments in the scene. And they came to believe that Jesus was the bread of life that came down from heaven. But the people could not keep this faith until the end. When they receive grace, they turn back and forget right away, and again make a grudge against God. This is what everyone has.

The great crowd knew that there was nothing to eat and the crowds who had been with Jesus for three days looked pitiful. The crowds walked with the Lord for three days fasting. The crowd loved the Lord so much. No one can fast. They are hungry for the word of the Lord because they are in the most urgent situation in all their lives, so they would like to receive a fast reply. So they will not hold food in their mouth for three days. 4,000 are somewhat smaller than 5,000.

There would have been a number that was unable to tolerate hunger for three days on the way. Faith is patience, and if you wait for a long time, the Lord will surely answer, but if you can not bear the time and give up and return, no miracles will happen. The Lord, who had watched for three days, felt compassion for those who did not go. No matter how hungry they were, if they were certain to believe that he was the Lord who saw the miracle of the last five loaves of bread and two fish miracle, they would be able to withstand any difficulties. This was what the Lord wanted.

In other words, the disciples complained about the problem of living with eating problems. At that time, toward the disgruntled disciples, the Lord said: "Do not you understand, because you have little bread? Do you still not understand? Do you not remember how many baskets you used to feed five thousand, and how many baskets you used to feed four thousand and seven loaves of bread?" This can be said to be a great reproach of unbelief that can not believe in the Lord.

Now the disciples were in the scene of the miracle of the five loaves of bread and two fish, but the disciples had forgotten the time now. In v. 4, we can not feed the crowds. We just said it was right to send the crowds back. It was not the answer Jesus wanted. We must realize through this miracle event. You should not say grudging or negative words. He who believes in the Lord must remember the events of the miracle. And if Jesus is Lord, people should know that about 4,000 people are nothing. The disciples, however, did not know the time of the miracle of the five loaves of bread and two fish and forgot it. Yet, in the miracle of the miracle, Andrew found the foods among the crowds and brought them directly to Jesus, which is not the case now. No one brought it to Jesus. It was enough to ask again. The disciples, who know the miracles of the five loaves of bread and two fish, had to say, of course, "Lord, here are seven loaves of bread and two fish. If you are in the power of the Lord, you will be able to feed these multitudes like the miracle before." So, after this problem, the disciples continued to have disbelief with the disciples and the crowds who were obsessed with the problem of eating and living without faith.

The disciples, who are hungry and complaining because they lacked the faith of their disciples, should see that they were ignorant who are not satisfied with what they have now. All that is said is that none of the hungry crowds are in front of the disciples' mouths. Whenever there is a problem, the disciples perceive only the problem at hand and do not see any more. It is said that Jesus' power has appeared at any time, but they has not got a vision of faith tied only to real problems.

It resembles many of us today. We can say that the Lord has given us so many things and that all things are the grace of God. If we come to realistic problems right now, our roots of faith will shake. Everyone ate them all and ate again in seven baskets. But the disciples sat down and said only negative words were in front of the Lord.

"Think of those who have spoken to you the word of God and have guided you, pay attention to the conclusion of their deeds and imitate their faith" (Hebrews 13: 7).

The Lord wants us to be a person who has a good influence on our faith. He always trusts in the Lord and wants to stand firm in words and conduct without shaking.

Finally, the Lord is the one who feeds us all the time. We must not forget that we know what we need and that the saints always feed and replenish the poor.

{Meditation Point}

1)How did Jesus lead me in my life? Have you not been interested in anything other than the form of eternal life, nor were you going to leave the Lord's bosom?
2)Are we always seeing that we have a problem with repeated problems? I hope we can look back on our appearance.
Let us meditate on the mercy of the Lord who feeds again.

CHAPTER 23

LORD WHO IS ABLE TO DO.

Mark 8: 22-26

"Once more Jesus put his hands on the man's eyes. Then his eyes were opened, his sight was restored, and he saw everything clearly (Mark 8:25)."

WE LIVE and try to solve all problems with our efforts. Sometimes you do not want to help and get help. But it seems easy to solve the problem of oneself, but it is not. We need wisdom to solve problems together rather than solve our own problems. There is no place in the world where there is no problem. There is always a problem wherever you go. If there is no problem, it will be the kingdom of God. Some say that humans live their whole lives and meet the problems and solve the problems and come to the end of their lives. If you solve one problem, you will encounter another problem. When you live well, you have health problems, and when you are healthy, you are faced with other problems.

That is because our life is so planned. If there is only one place in the Bible that does not have a problem, it may be the Garden of Eden that man dwells before sin. Adam and Eve have been driven out of the garden without such problems, and now they have come to a world where they have to live and solve everything themselves. Eve has a problem of conceiving a child, giving birth and nurturing it, a problem of home-keeping, and a problem in which Adam must solve all the necessary things for his own self.

Humans can not be free from problems. What is important? It is the wisdom that needs to be solved one by one and to overcome by finding the right solution in the problem that is not free. Those who face the most life are the people of reality. There are problems in front of the people. The Lord was buried in the matter and told how he could deal with the problems of struggling and conflicted people.

In front of the problem, we are trying to get rid of each other's mistakes.

The problem is that it creates another problem and teaches that one can lose the right judgment by being attached to the problem. The problem must be resolved wisely. With human power, the problem is not completely solved. Even if it is released, other problems may be caused by it. We must learn the wisdom of Jesus how Jesus dealt with the problem.

WHERE DID JESUS HEAL THE BLIND?

He fixed the blind man in Bethsaida. People brought the blind to Jesus. What is the problem of the blind? He will see right away. He wanted to be free from this problem of living with blindness and annoying him all his life. Then he came to hear rumors about Jesus from people and begged him to lead.

Invisibility is a spiritual problem as well as a physical disability problem. Jesus has always been interested in what people see. It was because there were many ignorant people in the spiritual world who did not know Jesus even though they were well looked after. Jesus was pleased to open these closed spiritual visions of compassion for both spiritually impaired and physically disabled. Before the problem, people become spiritual blind. The problem is that it hides a person's eyes and makes his judgment cloud. It induces people to look big enough to make a right judgment. So we will try to get a bigger problem out of the problem. It is a real problem for the Lord to look small and see the problem big, even though one should not look big on the problem but see the Lord big.

Those who lead the blind in the Lord did not try to solve the problem on their own. They did not find a member of the parliament or borrowed the power of the shaman with all human efforts. They have come to the Lord with problems. And they begged the Lord to touch him. Only the Lord can do it. We also say that you need to go to him to find a clue to solving problems.

HOW DID JESUS FIX THE BLIND EYE?

Hold your hand.

118

First, Jesus took hold of his hands to heal the blind eyes. The hold of the hand means that he has responded to the people's petition. People demanded that he touch it. The Lord responded to their demand that the hand of the blind was held by the hand of Jesus. Catching a hand is handed through the hand. Because the blind man can not see with his eyes, he was able to sense Jesus by touching Jesus' hand. The Lord has grabbed his hand with a caring heart toward the blind. He grabbed his hand with compassion. Just as you held your hand, we must feel the presence of Jesus in front of the problem. "Ah! The Lord wants to hold my hand before my problems." He says that the Lord must feel with him and experience him. We must believe and assure that the Lord still holds my hand and does not lay me down.

Guiding the blind

Second, he led the blind man out of the village. Why did the Lord go out of town without healing the blind in the village? It was quite a distance away from inside the village. He was able to heal right at the place, but he led him out of the blind. This should be considered in connection with the fact that he had caught the aforementioned hand.

The blind man can not see ahead. Then he grabbed the hand of the blind man and went out. The blind man finds out that his hands are drawn to the Lord and that he is going where he is going. What does this mean? It means to give everything to the Lord. I have to take my hand and lead me to believe in the Lord who guides me wherever I go and to follow Him to the end. The blind already has left everything to Him. So whatever I do, I was just letting the Lord do it. If you spit in your eyes and laid your hands on me, you will have no purpose, without hesitation, because he is the Lord. There was a growing history for him who believed in the problem. But the problem was not solved at once.

When he first laid his hands (the first ordination), the blind eye did not completely open. The Lord asked him. "What do you see?" Then the blind man said, "I see a man. I see trees and other things walking around." How would the tree walk? Here the tree means a person. Again, the person is completely invisible, and things like long sticks are wandering around. Even here is a great miracle. His eyes, which had never been seen before, are beginning to look a little hazy now. But the Lord was not satisfied here. More in-depth treatment was needed. So he is re-ordained. This ordination is the second one.

After the second laying of hands, this blind eye is completely opened. And now you can be sure?

The blind loudly says, "I see everything clearly." Everything in the 2nd Ordination has shown clearly. This miracle does not appear in any other Gospels. It is a miraculous ministry only in the Gospel of Mark. Jesus has ordained two times and opened the blind eye. You must not mistake the fact that Jesus has ordained two times since you have not completely healed it at first. In another Gospel, the eyes of the blind were fixed at once. And at some point he fixed it only with the Word. You should not doubt the power of Jesus with what you have divided and healed twice.

There is a special reason for dividing and repairing two times. The two ordinations must be seen as a complete ministry. Miracles have already happened through the first ordination. The first miracle alone has made the blind eye completely healed.

What we need to know is that the Lord will solve all the problems. The Lord is the one who has a definite finish until the problem is completely resolved. You must know that the Lord is holding on to the problem from beginning to end until the blind eye is lifted, not the midterm. In the process, the blind man was with the Lord until the end and showed faith in waiting and entrusting everything to the Lord. He left it to the Lord and waited until the Lord took responsibility for the matter and settled it. No matter how many problems are piled up like mountains, I hope that you will be a saint who has faith in the Lord who is releasing one by one.

"Great are the works of the Lord;
they are pondered by all who delight in them.
Glorious and majestic are his deeds,
and his righteousness endures forever.
Psalm 111: 2, 3"

"But everything should be done in a fitting and orderly way.
1 Corinthians 14:40"

{Meditation Point}

1)What did we do before the problems we encountered in our lives?
Have you ever begged to the Lord?

CHAPTER 24

A GENERATION WITHOUT FAITH

Mark 9: 14-29

"He replied, this kind can come out only by prayer (Mark 9:29)."

THIS GENERATION is called a generation without faith. It became a precious time for those who have faith. Everyone is biased and does not have the right faith. Wrong beliefs lead to wrong paths. There is a man who has spent his entire life in prison.

He was 15 years old when he first came to a juvenile court. With little greed, he steals a motorcycle in front of the house and sends the most important time of his life from the juvenile court. Since then, he has been repeating the arrest and release and is now over 50 years old. Listening to his words, he is sure that he believes in his youth. He said that the way he chose was a perfect way for him, refusing to listen to anyone and living as he stuck to his own thoughts.

What he thought and judged applied the word 'faith' to him. Is it true that faith is right? It is not. It is just an idea of oneself. That faith is a false belief. When a false faith dominated all of his, he would have gone the irreparable path.

The world lives by practicing what it believes like this. Every person has faith. But the Lord speaks to such people and the world as 'a generation without faith'. Why did the Lord say so? The present belief is a false belief, a false belief that chases after illusion and eventually destroys everything. The Lord then speaks through the text of what true faith is and why it must be owned.

WHAT IS IT TELLING US THROUGH THE WORD?

It can be seen that miracles work by faith. Faith is a must for miracles to appear.

Jesus was in some house of Capernaum. But friends brought a man with paralysis there. Jesus said in the Word, "See their faith." As a result, the daughter of a demon-possessed woman has also healed her, "Your faith is great." To be healed means to have faith.

It means that there must be a prayer of faith. Today, thousands of people pray for their problems. In the midst of this, those who still have faith should know that the work of miracles is taking place. Not only do we need the faith of the healed, but also the faith of the healer.

What does this mean? Those who pray for someone to heal or pray for the healing and restoration of others need to know that faith is needed. In short, it can be called 'the faith of the missionary.' In other words, it means that people who do the Lord's work also need faith. Without faith, I can not do the Lord's work. Those who want to have the faith of a missionary need some attitude for faith.

EVERYTHING IS POSSIBLE IF GOD IS WITH US.

First, you must first have faith that if God is with us, you will make everything possible. Everything is possible for the Lord. He is the Lord who controls the heavens and earth and asserts all human life and death. The Lord is the master of the world. It means that there is a limit to what we do as a person, but we need a certain conviction of faith that is possible if the Lord is with us. It means to have faith that you can do if you believe in God.

TRUST IN THE POWER OF GOD.

The second is the belief that God's power will be manifested through him if he is fully dependent on the power of the Lord. I can not, but it is important to have faith that God is capable of doing it through me. Paul said in Philippians 4 that "I can do all things through him who gives me strength" (13). In another version, "there is nothing I can not do through him who gives us the power." And recently, the Bible translated for the modern man says, "In the one who makes me into me now, I can do everything." What does this mean? It is that faith should not deprive the noblest value. Some people think that if they believe, can they really do everything? There are those who say that believing is not done. This is a wrong idea. Everything is possible in faith. There is nothing impossible in him who gives power to the Word.

This means that if you have faith, you will have the ability to overcome any problems or difficulties.

THE LORD WHO IS WITH ME

Third, you must believe that the Lord is with me. When I look at one person, it is scarce, weak and often falls. I am at a low place, but our God is high. The Lord who created heaven and earth is with me, the smallest in the world. He is accompanied by me. Faith means to believe in this Lord. The Immanuel is dependent on the Lord.

PROVIDENCE OF GOD

Fourth, all that is done is to be sure that the Lord has done it. If I believed that the Lord was with me and what appeared to be power in it, I should admit that it was not obtained by doing well but by the power of God. It is in this case that a person often falls into the swamp of pride. It is because I am. I am good because I pray, and because I am outstanding, the idea that history has taken place is spiritual pride. I am not doing well, but the Lord has worked through me, and I have been used only as an instrument in the Lord's work.

In Acts 3:12, Peter fixed a man sitting at the temple gate. People have noticed Peter in all this marvelous work. His power seemed magnificent as if he had fixed a sick man. But what does Peter say to them? Do not pretend to have walked this man by his own power, but Jesus has healed it. He has turned all glory to the Lord to look to Jesus and believe.

This is faith. At the center of our faith am not I, but the Lord. You must know this. It is by God's power that the sickness is healed. We should know that we have not been healed by our intentions.

I'M USING YOU AS A TOOL

Fifth, faith believes that the Lord is still using me as a tool. Even now, the Lord must be convinced that he is using someone like me. We are the tools of the Lord. We are like vessels that the Lord uses. We are not good enough to be used, but we need to be thankful for the grace of the Lord who is using us, even though it is lacking.

BELIEVE TO THE END

Sixth, faith must protect to the end. It is faith that is not always changing. Faith that is praised is faith that does not give up. It is faith to depend on the Lord to the end. How then can we keep our faith to the end? It is the power of prayer. Without prayer, it is hard to keep faith to the end. In Mark 6, the Lord entrusted and dispatched his disciples in pairs to preach. After they return to the Lord, they report their evangelism. It was really what the Lord had taught us to do, and the devil was leaving, and the sick people were hearing that there was a healing work. It is because of what the Lord taught us.

HERE ARE THREE REASONS FOR THE MIRACLE WORK.

First, because he obeyed the Lord's command to go, he sent it to preach, so he believed the word and went through history.

Second, the Lord sent and did not leave them irresponsibly. The power of the Lord is with them.

The one who supported the disciples who worked in the front was the Lord in the rear. The Lord manipulated everything from behind.

Third, there was a faith of obedience. This obedience is obedience to the Word. It depends on the Word. Until this time, the disciples were able to experience the work of faith because they relied on the Lord. The disciples didn't do that. We need to know one fact. We are not special people who are capable. We are received by the power of God and are used by the Lord. If anyone is a faithful man, he is the one who exercises power through him. The disciples mistook this. The miracles happened because they were really capable. It is not because of them, but because of the power of the Lord. Because we have been doing ourselves for a long time, we must abandon the idea that we can do it ourselves. Even now, if the Lord is not with us, there is nothing we can do. We should not think of it as having power. A generation without faith means this generation. They all depend on themselves. In my experience, it is my belief that those who think that I can do what I have in my own knowledge are a generation without faith.

Through this, we now know the present state of my faith. What about you guys? Do you live with an unbelieving generation? Or are you standing before the Lord in faithful generations?

We have to look at ourselves through the Word that we do not really believe, but are not mistaken as having faith. It was not possible to try to repair a man who believed in himself and suffered his disciples. It all got to the bottom. He felt a human limit. This man did not do faith from the beginning. He worked without praying. A person without faith does not pray and always does his work. You must know that it can be a weakness to the devil.

{Meditation Point}

1)What is the difference between believing in me and in the Lord?
This generation we live in is a generation without faith. God tells us to have faith. Therefore, the standard of our faith must be Jesus Christ, not me.

CHAPTER 25

A COIN PICKED UP IN A FISH STOMACH

Matthew 17: 24-27

"But so that we may not offend them, go to the lake and throw out your line. Take the first fish you catch; open its mouth and you will find a four-drachma coin. Take it and give it to them for my tax and yours (Matthew 17:27)."

ASKED ABOUT the breadth of the kingdom of God, it replied: For those who are pure in heart, the place where there is no end is the kingdom of God. It is the kingdom of God that is narrower than a needle in a person whose heart is rough.

The world becomes more miserable as the day approaches, and the affection between the people becomes parched. It is an era where people can not trust people. In the same way in the Bible, when the Lord was there, people were hardened by sin and the door of the heart was not opened. The history of apostasy was sustained, and it was such an era that human-centered and idol-centered time prevailed in God-centered faith. Jewish religious leaders made law provisions more restrictive than caring for the people, making them the means to control the people, and the people who did not find true leaders in it were spiritually thirsty. Living in a society without acknowledgment means living in a world where people have walled up and are separated from each other. The dialogue between the parent and the child is cut off, the family communication; the neighboring fellowship is cut off.

This is also because the nature of man has been fundamentally corrupted, and the roots and flows of sin flowing in it have not been cut off, and it is possible to see that it continues to grow as the generations are repeated.

In this situation, it is first necessary to the children of the Lord to restore broken human relationships in God. It is a way of reaching out to those who have stumbled around and restoring the relationship of love that the Lord has spoken.

God's people have a passionate and clean. They love and think of one another, and raise them up when they fall. So the people of God must be seen unlike the people of the world. Everyone is born different. Even the twins are similar in appearance but different. God so created all the people of this world. God is love and loves his chosen people. He is our most beloved. We must know that we are different from the people of the world. The Lord is always on our side. The fact that someone is on my side is a great comfort. It would be a great help if I could understand and help my situation on my part. The Lord is such a being for us. Just as a needle follows a thread, it should not be forgotten that Christians and the Lord are closer than the flesh of the world.

WHO IN THE WORD COMES TO PETER AND SAYS? AND WHAT IS ITS CONTENT?

The disciples and the Lord arrived at Capernaum. But as soon as they arrived there were people who appeared to them. It was the tax collectors. These were the people who collected the taxes. In the Word, it is said to be a recipient of half a shekel. He is not the one who gives half a shekel, but the one who receives it. The monetary unit called 'shekel' was learned in Bible study time. Where is the monetary unit used? It was not used in everyday life but used only in the temple. A temple is a holy place. In this holy place, money that is common in the world should not be used. Since the temple is the place where God is, there was a need for especially distinguished money, the currency being shekel. He was a half-shekel of the temple tax collector. 'Semi-shekel' is Di Drachma. Judah's leaders paid taxes only to adult men to maintain or manage the temple.

One drachma at the time was a worker's wage for the day. Two days' wages are to pay for the temple. At that time, it was a lot of money. It was the discipline that people set to make a half shekel.

It is a burden on the person who is difficult to afford. Moreover, the disciples were poor people who had none.

You have to pay two days' tax. Peter replies, "Of course," the tax collector stopped all the time. When tax collectors come and say about taxes, they are quick to pay taxes. The disciples are the same person, which means that it is natural to cast a castle.

Peter answered only that he would make it instantaneously. There was not a penny in the water right now. He was worried. Where does he go and does two jobs? Going forward, it was a problem to go back.

The tax collectors were bright men. They were treated as sinners and ignored among the people. Because he had collected taxes, he lived more abundantly than others, but he received the resentment of the people because he went to the poor and forcibly collected them. When Peter came to tell him to pay taxes, Peter initially said that he would pay for his self-esteem.

WHAT DOES JESUS SAY TO THIS PETER THAT HE COMFORTS HIM?

Jesus had already known Peter's mind that he was coming home because of the downcast. He was the one who read his mind with the expression of what you were worrying about. Jesus knew the anxieties and worries of Peter and said comforting words. There is a saying in the Word, 'Jesus first said'. Jesus did not ask. He did not wait until Peter first discussed it. Because He already knew his worries, He asked him first. The Lord knew in advance what could not be said. This is the word of Jesus' comfort. "Peter, what do you think? Who will pay the tax if the king takes the tax, children of the king or the people pay?" He wanted to know Peter's thoughts. If the king wants to collect the tax, will the children of the king pay the tax? Or shall the people yield? It is. Who is obligated to pay taxes? It is. Of course, the obligation to pay taxes is not on the children of the king, but of the people.

The people shall take charge of the kingdom. The king and his children do not have to pay taxes. Now the rulers and children have to pay taxes, but then the status of the king was absolute. It was the owner of the country. The king does not need to pay taxes because he is the master. Of course, the children have nothing to say. In Peter's reply, the Lord replied, "Are not your children exempt?" This is the question of what is your identity now. Is Peter now a servant of the people? Or is he the son of the King, Jesus Christ? You asked for your current location. If Peter is a people, he must pay taxes, but if he is the king's child he will not have to worry about taxes. He was the one who said that taxes must be paid out as a people. "Caesar's righteousness is to Caesar, and God's righteousness to God." Paul also said that the Saints should pay taxes. The problem is that God prepares and prepares all things for his children in advance. If you are a child of God, it is important to leave everything to God and wait with boldness. It is natural for the Lord to receive an exemption from Peter for his children. You are a child of God, so do not be discouraged because God will take care of your money.

Go to the lake and go fishing. And unconditionally, the first thing is to catch fish and open its mouth. One coin will come out of its mouth, and you will have to take it and give it to them as a tax. And if it is the money, you and I will be enough for you. Jesus is now speaking an incredible Word. Since Peter is a fisherman, he is a man of history to catch fish. The Lord has saved Peter's skill. The Lord is the one who makes bread with stones even though he is still. It's easy to get a coin, but Peter did it. What can you do is catch fish? If you obey me as I say, you will save Peter's skills and use miracles.

A man without faith can not make a decision. How can you expect to find a coin in the belly of the first fish you catch? Some people do not believe how such things can happen. But if it was the Lord, it was possible.

There is this story. It is the story that a man sought strawberries in the mountains in the harsh desire to hear the wish of his mother. Strawberries are summer fruit, not winter. By the way, he believed that he would be there and went to the mountain. The same is true of Peter. Because Jesus said so, he saved his job and went fishing, and in the end, he was able to save a coin in the fish's belly according to the Lord's words. With this coin, he got two things. One was to keep his duty as a people, and the other as a child of God, to be sure that he was the one he loved. And finally, He experienced his faith. When he was in distress and worry, he was able to look back on himself. Do I have a skill in fishing? The Lord has tried to live it well and to obey the Lord's Word and to challenge with faith and experience miracles. Peter, who could not catch a fish at night, threw a net in order to experience miracles on the seafront and to give him the courage and strength to depend more on the Lord.

The Lord is the abundant One. Not a half shekel. Just one shekel of money was in its stomach. A shekel is the wage of a worker four days. A shekel was enough money for the castle of the Lord and Peter. It is the Lord who fills the amount of faith for those who have faith. it free from all the problems that plagued Peter when there was a history of obedience to the Word of the Lord, not worrying about a matter. He who is pure in heart is the kingdom of God. He who believes and listens has the privilege of being a child of God. But those who worry, especially those who are deprived of the things of the world, forget that they are children of God, and feel that all the things of the world are as narrow as the needles. Peter initially felt that way, but as the Lord understood and solved Peter's heart, he was able to gain many things at the same time (as a people, by raising the right-face, having the privilege of being a child, you know the location of yourself.

{Meditation Point}

1)Did you ever worry about material problems like Peter in your life? Have you been ignored for being poor?
2)Meditate on the Lord's delicate care to get everything. Let us meditate on the Lord who is responsible for my life.

CHAPTER 26

GO TO SILOAM POND AND WASH!

John 9: 1-7

"Go! He told him, wash in the pool of Siloam (this word means Sent). So the man went and washed, and came home seeing (John 9:7)."

IN THE United States, there was a time of discrimination due to skin color.

Although the discrimination due to skin color has been alleviated much by the steady efforts of the society at various levels, the skin color caused much discrimination even a few decades ago, causing a lot of social problems. God is not discriminating by man's skin color. What should be the life of the people? It is not the will of God that their lives become infinitely poor, low, and socially unacceptable. The people are socially weak and powerful. Why can it say this? They are being dragged away and taken away to receive it if they are oppressed as if they are nothing on the surface, but if faith in God is entered into them, they can live as a victor of life. Is the problem a faith in God, in the people? If there is a pure faith toward God, it means that the people can pioneer the era and stand as a leader. He is the one who changes people. Do not forget that you are a person who changes people so that you can do the great work of God.

WHO WAS HE WHEN HE CAME OUT? HOW DID HE LIVE?

It was when Jesus was walking down the road. As he walks down the road, the Lord met with the blind man from the days of birth. He did not look ahead. He was a blind as soon as he was born. One of the important functions of the human body is that there is no visual function. From this day on, the blind man had never seen the Lord. He just saw the blind man from the first time when he went to the road. The disciples said to the Lord, "Whose sin is this man caused to blindness? Himself or is it because of his parents?" They were so sorry for him. He was born with some sins, and asked what he should do to the sons of the parents, who should have suffered any sins.

At that time the Jews taught, 'Without sin, there is no pain.' Whatever happened, he had an obsession with the fate that things would happen because of his sins. It is a story about pain and about the cause. People had thought that all the painful phenomena were the result of sin that caused God's wrath. But this was people's thoughts, not God's thoughts. People thought that the cause of their suffering was the sins they had built. But it was a wrong idea. Jesus wanted to blind and fix the blind when he was going to correct this wrong idea.

The Lord said that in the fallen, sinful world, people are sick, bad things happen often, and evil things happen without any reason. It does not happen because of sin. We are living in a sinful world, thinking that everything is related to sin, and that is not what the Lord sees. What does the Lord say? It is not because of the sin of himself or of his parents that this man has not seen his eyes since he was born, but that he is to manifest what God is doing. He said. It is not that we have not seen for the sake of sin, but that we have not come forward to show God's work. It is a fateful idea that I am suffering because of the sins of my parents.

Chinese character, 'Destiny: 運(Un)命(Myong)' is a life-giving experience. It is a Chinese word that we all know, but there is also this Chinese language. It is a 'death: 殞(Un)命(Myong)'. It is a 'death-worthy person' in the 'fortune to die'. In the latter mortality, the life name means the life that has already ended. I am already determined life. The 'death name' in the 'life-giving luck' is something to look forward to, but the 'death name' means the case that the hope is lost. Those who have been blind since the day of death have already died. Hope was completely lost. No one was on his side. It was thoroughly lonely and isolated. Though man said that it is because of sin, he found a desire that was left in the sight of the Lord, even though it was a life that had already ended. The hope is to live the life of reversal.

So far we have lived in fate, but now it is time for the glory of God to be revealed through blindness. Jesus said, "We must do the work of the One who sent me in the days when time is still low." At night, no one can do that. The Lord is not trying to connect sin and everything, but rather expecting God to do what he will do in the future. God's work is to send Christ and bear witness of the gospel.

It has opened the way through Christ. It is daytime to save people through the Lord. To this end, Jesus came to the light of the world. Those who are desperate and think that everything is over are those who live in destiny. It means the people who give up on their own and give up on being pulled away.

It is people who are caught in fate. The saints should not live that way. I need a position to forget all the past and to wait for God to guide my future.

Jesus also solved the problem of sin by healing many sick people. In the process Samaritan woman was asked about the past, and sickness was declared forgiveness. But the blind did not. He is not suffering for sin, but is trying to heal him in order to free him from destiny just to reveal God's glory. We can be in difficulty regardless of our will. That is important. It is time to rely on the Lord.

HOW DID JESUS OPEN THE EYES OF THE BLIND?

First, He gave the Word. The Word must be entered first. There is nothing as important as the Word. You should not lean on something other than the Word. The gift of the Word is the most blessed and one of the best gifts. The blind man received the Word first. It is Jesus who came to the light of the world. It was the brightest light that was most needed in the blind. What he needed was to see the light.

Jesus told himself that he is the light of the world. We must first know who Jesus is to me. How did the Lord come to you? There are many differences between people. Some have met the Lord during the sickness, some have met when they are in trouble, and others vary according to various circumstances. This blind man met when he could not see. First, he was ready to believe and accept the Word by calling it Light. The Lord spit on the ground and made the clay to go to the pool of Siloam and wash it.

Because the blind man can not see the way, he could not but leave his body to the Lord. And he commanded him to go to the Siloam pond and wash it. Siloam is just a well. It is a place where drinking water exists. It is not a place of special healing like Bethesda Pond. It is a common spring. He went to such a place and washed his eyes. Nobody guided this blind man to Siloam.

He just had to go by himself. Our faith is like washing our eyes, depending on the Word of God, to go to Siloam pond. Faith is that every day a new spiritual eye has. We must renew our spiritual eyes as we see the Word and pray. For that, spiritual Siloam must always be near us. Our Siloam is a church. It should be where the spring water of the Word comes out. If we do not renew our spiritual eyes, our eyes become increasingly dull in spirituality. When it gets dull, people often find and rely on others. We are dependent on people and listen to people. We must hold onto the Word and go to Siloam well. He is the light of the world, and he who is like me can open his eyes. I will go to Siloam Pond by believing. We must hold on to the Word and rely on it. We should go to spiritual Siloam often. It is a place to experience the power of the Word. It is a place to be experienced when you believe what you said and history has just happened.

A spiritual experience without a Word is dangerous. Those who experience the Wordless experience believe in seeing with eyes. Even if you do not have a word, at first you have a human-centered experience. But later on, you follow human and eventually leads to idols. The Word of God comes into me. Every word of the Bible sometimes comes into me and becomes one in my thoughts and in reason. The Word is rooted in my heart. And then the power of the Word will appear in me and in my life. And you will experience the power of the Word for yourself. We do not rely on people, but God's approach to me through the Word and experience of God. We heard the blind without seeing. He held the word and went to Siloam and washed it. Then he could see. When we rely on the Word, all the fateful past that torments us has left us and become a new person.

The blind life so far has been a life that has been lived by its own destiny, but life in the future has been transformed into a life that is lifted up to the spiritual eye as well as the physical eye and lives for the Word of God.

{Meditation Point}

1)How many words do I hold the verses of Bible?

135

CHAPTER 27

THOSE WHO HAS A KIDNEY INFECTION

Luke 14: 1-6

"Jesus asked the Pharisees and experts in the law, is it lawful to heal on the Sabbath or not?"(Luke 14:3)

DISEASE IN humans is the most inevitable problem in life. There is no one in the world that has no disease. Everyone suffers from more than one illness and lives through it. Everyone is suffering from more than one illness, and lives by disease. Aging is also one of the diseases. Human aging causes various abnormal phenomena in the body, and the aged body can not adapt to it, so that the disease causes the person to die. Disease is the result of human's original sin. It is the eternal homework that fallen mankind must solve. There are neighbors who are suffering from this fundamental problem and are neglected. We can meet many of them who have been healed miraculously from disease by faith.

Among them, one will overcome the disease and experience healing. Sickness is the price of the original sin of man, but it can still be said to be a kind of experiential place that can show the grace and mercy of God to man. Anyone who enters this experience will have the opportunity to meet God through the healing of the disease. Jesus came to this earth and preached the gospel of the kingdom of God, and at the same time, it was the ministry of healing. Many sick people go to the Lord to be healed and receive the gospel on the spot and be saved. The disease came as an opportunity to best accept the gospel of God.

It is said that the hospital is the place where the most evangelism can be done easily and the ministry is vigorous today. It is a place where healthy people do not come and people who are suffering from disease are gathered. What is most needed for them is that they need someone to save them from this moment of pain. If you tell the story of many corrections and healing in the Bible, many people will easily open the door of heart to the Lord. When the flesh becomes weak, the grace of God is to be found in the presence of God.

People are no exception. They are just weak people. Those who live with the sickness of the heart and the sickness of the flesh are all people. The Lord meets such people and gives them together.

WHO CAME OUT OF THE TEXT AND WHAT DISEASES DID HE HAVE?

The disease should be diagnosed and treated correctly. If you know the cause and treat it, you will not come back again. The Lord knew what the root of the disease was. Today, we want to know about some kinds of diseases and their spiritual meaning. The Jews regarded the Sabbath, the Day of Atonement, the lunar month, and the fifth season festivals as very important. They did nothing to do that day, but tried to live literally. On the Sabbath Jesus went to the house of a man of the leader among the Pharisees, and was invited to eat. However, people brought a person who was suffering from some kind of illness on the spot. This is what Jesus did on the Sabbath to bring him to temptation. It has come without waiting for grace. The Sabbath is a day of grace, but it has come to worship in trial.

JESUS WANTED TO HEAL SOMEONE WHO WAS SICK, REGARDLESS OF THEIR INTENTIONS.

Jesus healed the Sabbath day. He has healed those who have some kind of disease. The Pharisees looked at the scene and asked the Lord. Jesus was not disturbed by their words, and said, "If any of you have slain his son or ox in the well, will he not soon draw them on the Sabbath?" The Pharisees who were there did not answer the Lord's wisdom. Why did Jesus heal the sickness?

FIRST YOU NEED TO KNOW ABOUT SOME KINDS OF DISEASE.

It is a name that does not exist in any other Bible. It is commonly known as one of the nephritis. The function of the kidney is not good and the water is not decomposed.

It is said to be a kind of phenomenon that when water is sent to the urethra, it is not abnormally removed from the urethra to the outside. The moisture in the body is 75%. When you eat food, you need to absorb as much water as you need to absorb and make blood, and unnecessary things should be discharged out of the body. However, the water does not go to one place. There is blood in the body, but it swells when water comes in. If you continue to drink water, your body becomes swollen and worse. It is a disease caused by a weak function of the body.

The function of one part of the body is paralyzed and it is a state that can not be properly touched. This is the case where one side is not treated. To be healthy, we have to balance, but we can not. It is hard to maintain balance. Every person has a particularly weak part. If the body is bad, the symptoms will appear in the weak part. Perhaps the disease is like a spiritual disease. If you see a person who falls spiritually, you can not keep one side. Several diseases are similar to those of spiritual disease. So it becomes helpless and everything is twisted. Thinking is also curved. It is not bright. There is always a disease, so the expression is dark.

If we have this weak part, we must come to Jesus. That way you can get treatment. The person who came out to the Lord in the text should, for one reason or another, assume that he made the right decision by the fact that it came out. It means that it is important that the Pharisees come out to the Lord in order to restore their weak body, which is not important, whether it came from the force of the Pharisees or whether it came out voluntarily. It does not matter how we come to the Lord. There is hope in us, even in the presence of the Lord. Whatever form of worship you have, you can be pleased with God only by the fact that you came to participate in worship.

It is not necessary to distinguish between the Sabbath and the other weekdays to come to the Lord. It is a life-saving thing and should not distinguish time and place. The Lord did not distinguish between time and place, and did not postpone, if it were to save life. It is He who has accomplished history on that very day. We must also follow the Lord. It is not the act of faith that says to keep the Sabbath day holy nothing to do good things. The Sabbath is a day of salvation. The Sabbath is the day of saving life.

WHY DID HE REMEDY THE DISEASE? LET'S SEE WHAT THAT MEANS.

Several diseases are chronic diseases.

It is not a sudden illness, but a fatal disease that digs into the fragile part of the body invisible for a long period of time, paralyzing its function and eventually leading to death. The function of the body is getting weaker. This is just frightening. For us, chronic diseases like tiredness can not bring vitality to our faith life, as we do to make people tired and unable to do anything. The Lord wants to know and heal such people.

The Lord wants the curled life to expand. He makes us perfect. No matter how far our life has been twisted and distorted, we have to come to the Lord, who is strong in his frailty, because the Lord is in charge of the fragile portion. It is the Lord who strengthens us with weakness. Just as we should not put chronic diseases, such as some kinds of diseases, long, we must solve our spiritual problems so that they no longer take root in us. You should not postpone the problem to be solved. Now is the time to get it fixed. The Lord was not the one to put back any circumstances. He was the one who solved it.

It is the Lord who solves all situations, not the ones who settle according to the circumstances. He did not judge the kind of disease. He healed all the sick people. The dead also came to life. The Lord is one who does not miss every single problem. This Lord has not given up his ministry anywhere he goes.

He was the one who thought this was my work. We need this attitude. No matter what, I should not give up thinking that it is my job. People always have a condition. However, the Lord did not give up or delay the work because of any reasons. People were obsessed with deep-seated thoughts that they should not work if they were on the Sabbath. This is a stereotype. I believed that I should not work. It was because of this belief that this false belief had been a hindrance to walking toward faith in the wrong way.

The stereotype is like pinned paper. I have to remove the paper, but I can not remove it because of the deep pin. In the end, it will force you to tear the paper. It should be noted that false stereotypes can lead to wrong behavior and results. It was a stereotype not to work on the

Sabbath. Let's go for the Lord. Rather, it has resulted in the disregard and contempt of the preciousness of man's soul.

The Lord was the one who perceived stereotypes. The Lord does not have stereotypes toward us. "Why do you keep looking like that?"

The Lord has completely changed people's minds and showed that they can work proudly on the Sabbath day. The disciples' stereotypes (they can not get anything because of the desert or they will all die because of the storm in the sea) didn't make them to go forward.

Do not go near because the demon has been heard, because the lepers are cursed and should not go their home. These are examples of stereotypes. He changed everything and freely judged and acted without being tied to anything.

The Lord did not notice. He was not conscious of the eyes of those who blamed the Lord. Sometimes we want to imitate this attitude of the Lord. There are a lot of people in front of the situation. We look at people who are more talented than I am.

We spend too much attention on who is around us. I am nervous about who comes in today's meeting, what kind of group comes. But the Lord was always standing up everywhere. He was always full of confidence. The confidence gave faith and instilled reality in many people. He did not choose where he was, at any time, or anybody else.

{Meditation Point}

1)What diseases have you been bothering me so far? Everyone has one weak spot. What is the weak part? What if there is an obstacle to your spiritual life?
2)Do you have any problems you have stayed in so far?

CHAPTER 28

LORD'S HEART TOWARD THE WOMAN

Luke 13: 10-17

"When Jesus saw her, he called her forward and said to her, Woman, you are set free from your infirmity. Then he put his hands on her, and immediately she straightened up and praised God (Luke 13:12-13)."

THE ROLE of the woman in the ministry of the Lord and in the ministry of the Early Church should be seen as occupying an important position. In the Gospels, it was the women who helped by the ministry of the Lord and his disciples. They have materially helped the Lord and his companions do not have trouble maintaining a livelihood to witness the gospel. And in the early churches, women like Tabitha and Lydia were zealous for the good and evangelism of the church.

As a result, the church was able to cope well with mission work internally without difficulty. In the ministry of the gospel it was a woman will occupy an important position. What position is a woman on? It was a being that could not insist on rights properly in Jewish society. At home, she had to devote herself to honoring husband, nurturing children, and helping with housework. It was not a society that greatly emphasized the existence of women. The presence of a woman was a weakness, and it needed protection. But unlike the intent of this love of the Lord, the Jews had different perspectives. They are not interested in love but have seen people in a repressive way of applying the law and redeeming it.

The Jews had a lot of interest in the sins of others than their own sin. It is not seeing oneself but seeing others. But the Lord said that all need repentance. The present condition of Israel was like a fig tree that could not bear fruit. There was no fruit for three years. And to give them one more chance through Jesus Christ toward those without hope. Jesus is the last chance to be saved. When you gave up, the hope was cut off. If you reject Him, you will lose the opportunity to be saved forever.

WHOM DID JESUS HEAL ON THE SABBATH DAY?

On the Sabbath there was a woman who had been haunted by evil spirits for 18 years and was curled. Looking at the kind of woman the Lord has mercy on his soul. And he said, "Woman, thou hast settled in thy illness (12), and laid his hands on her, and she straightened up and glorified God" (Luke 13: 10-13) (in case of the spinal cord), and the woman who is standing up alone and unable to lift her head in prayer, has been healed. The demon is dominating the body and mind of a person so that normal people can not live a full life. Think that you have lived for 18 years instead of one or two years. Not only that, but also the view of the world was twisted and curled.

While the desperate thought served as a curse and blame the world.

But what made her feel sicker was the unfathomable gaze around her. She was shocked by her physical and mental problems, and she wasn't very proud of her life. People did not give a place because the demons were in her when they saw her.

Especially the Jews had wrong thoughts. They also forbid reading 'Tora'. In the first century, Rabbi Elijah did not admit the woman's right to say, "It is better to burn the torah rather than let the women read the torah." And the Jews prayed for three things when they wake up in the morning. The first one is not to be a Gentile, the second is not to be a slave, and the third is that he did not make me a woman. Husband always had the right to divorce, but the woman had no right to divorce first under any circumstances. No one admitted that right.

Moreover, it was unfortunate that she had not dealt with anyone who had been a woman for a long time and was unable to live a normal life because of the spirit of a terrible demon. The people's gaze was so harsh, but the Lord was different.

What did the Lord say when he saw her? This statement tells us about Jesus' view for woman. It was called 'the daughter of Abraham.' Jesus was the one who respects women. In the same descendants of Abraham who would treat her. And she pities her body, which is curly. So he laid his hands on the back of her head and drove out demons.

LET US THINK ABOUT THE LOVE OF LORD WHO HEALED THE SICKNESS.

She was born in a strict patriarchal society, lived with an unusual body, and all her troubles, which were suffering from double-damages, were solved at once in front of the Lord. The woman came to the synagogue even though her body was suffering. It is only a feeling to meet the Lord that she came to receive treatment despite the Sabbath. What came on the Sabbath is the act of faith. She has not looked at people. She was not conscious of the person's gaze but came to the chapel in a spirit of meeting only the Lord.

You should not be burdened with coming out of the church. We should be pleased to know that we are going to church.

All saints do not come to church in a healthy body. There is always a problem whether the body hurts or the heart aches. When there is such a problem, we must first have a desire for the house of the Lord. The heart of desiring the church, the desire for the word should not change. You are such a woman, you have settled in your sickness. It was already prepared and it was fixed. He does not just return those who seek Him by faith, but he hears them as the best. The work of this mercy of the Lord continues.

LET US THINK ABOUT WHETHER WE HAVE THE SAME MIND AS THE LEADER OF THE SYNAGOGUE.

Our hearts should not be the hearts of the synagogue rulers. We had to rejoice together. We had to thank God for a soul to be saved and to be liberated. But the rulers did not. The rulers should rejoice together, but condemn the woman, judge. They are accusing the Lord of breaking the Sabbath day. We must thank the one soul in heaven for salvation, and let the soul return to the bosom of the Lord, however they do not come to the joy, the ruler of the synagogue also criticize her.

The synagogue ruler did not see the woman only once. The ruler may have seen the appearance every week in the synagogue. But the ruler did not pray for her, but rather condemned. This is the person who is responsible for the synagogue. He blamed the Lord for what he had done that he could not do. If this person is not one person in the synagogue but more than one person, no one would want to come to the chapel. We must be the one who has the heart of the Lord than the heart of the synagogue ruler. The Lord speaks against the words of the synagogue ruler.

Then the Lord answered and said, "You hypocrites, each of you on the Sabbath unleashed from his ox, donkey, or horse, and does not go and feed the water?" (15) Then the daughter of Abraham, (16) when Jesus said this, all the opponents were ashamed, and all the crowds rejoiced in all the glorious things which he did! "(Luke 13: 15-17)

In the Qumran sect, the Sabbath ruled that livestock could travel about 900 meters to feed grass. It is a certain consideration for cattle and horse. However, it is not enough to say that it is a matter of healing people, but it is neither cattle nor horse nor man. Human is better than beast. And this woman is too important to be healed on the Sabbath. The Jewish law is a contradictory law that was strict to her if it was generous to animals. Jesus said, "Are not you worthy?" This means that you must do it. It does not mean that you can fix it, but you have to fix it. You must be involved in saving lives, and you can not make a distinction between the Sabbath day and the other day. The Sabbath is the day of the Lord and the day of life. It is the holy day God has given for the benefit of man. On the Sabbath day we must be able to do well. If you have a sick person, you should have visiting and prayer. If there is a saint who does not come out of the test, it is Sabbath. The meaning of the recognition date should be properly defined.

{Meditation Point}

1)Have you ever been discriminated against because of being a woman? Have you ever been treated as a socially weak person?
2)How did I spend the Sabbath (Sunday)? Did not you feel burdened by my church or lost my time?

CHAPTER 29

THE LORD, WHO GAVE HOPE TO THE FAMILY WITH LAZARUS

John 11: 17-26

"Jesus said to her, I am the resurrection and the life, He who believes in me will live even though he dies; and whoever lives and believes in me will never die. Do you believe this? (John 11:25-26)."

THE PROBLEM of death in humans is inevitable. Even if you have a sickness to die, you will do all sorts of treatments before you die. You will try fasting prayers.

Death is a fate that man can not avoid. Everyone in the world is to die. Theologian Karl Barth said, death is nearer to some, far away to some, but what is evident is getting closer to us.

The death comes to us as time flows. Our remaining life is getting worse and worse. The one who runs for death is the one who runs toward the end. If any one in the family is dead, the death of all the family will lead to sorrow and despair. There is no hope left. And if one person in the family is despairing, the hearts of all remaining family members are not at ease.

If the father, the wife, the child, any one are in grief, the whole will be affected. It is important to know that not only death but other problems also make people despair. Death gives the greatest sorrow, but difficult problems in many families equally despair. The Lord has come for those who are right. He came to be a desire for those who mourn for death and for other desperate problems.

It is said that the age of modernity is collapsing. Authority as a parent and discontinuity of conversation among family members play a major role in generating many societal side effects. Home is the minimum basic unit of society. The collapse of the family can be seen as a trigger for the society to move into an unstable society. What does the Lord say? He restores a wounded and destroyed family. No matter how great sadness may be in the family, you should know that the

Lord is compassionate, binds the wound, and restores the ruined family. People's homes are collapsing. The family members of the people are scattered about by the collapse, and the family members are going wrong ways. The Lord comes to a family today and solves the problem of great sorrow in that family. You must know that the Lord is the Lord of resurrection that overcame death.

WHO IS THE FAMILY FROM THE TEXT AND WHAT IS THE PROBLEM WITH THAT FAMILY?

Lazarus, the only man in the family of Lazarus, died. Lazarus' sisters were Mary and Martha. They were Jesus' companions, as did the most faithful of the Lord who appeared frequently in the Bible. The Bible does not mention their parents. As they relate to each other, they were living with each other as they were responsible for their own lives. But there was a serious problem with this poor family. Lazarus, a man who has to play the most important role in the home of a brother and sister who can not depend on anyone, was seriously ill and died. This sister, who was close to the Lord, informed Jesus of the use of Lazarus, who was sick.

When Jesus heard this news, he was delayed two more days. When he left for Bethany, Lazarus was not a man of this world. It has been four days since it was buried in the grave. The funerals were all finished. To the sister who lost her beloved family, the Lord arrived very late, unexpectedly. Martha, the older sister who went out to meet Jesus, says: "If he had been here, he would not have died," he said. Mary would have been able to live if he had been here in the same way." What does this mean? You can see that you have recognized and believed to some extent the power of the Lord. If you are the Lord, you can heal the disease, but the dead can not. Is the word that limits the ability of the Lord? What will you do until death? It is like saying.

It means that the problem of the death of a person can never be solved. When you die, everything is done. Lazarus' death was a problem of putting the whole family in a state of failure and frustration. It is the problem of life that even demolishes the desire to live even a living person. Home is a precious place. But the family collapsed because of one person. In the mind of man, that assumption is already over. It is a tragic assumption that can not be expected anymore. The Lord felt pity for the sisters who were left and tears for those who were grieving. Even with the Lord, it was God's tears for humans who are desperate for the present problems.

HOW DID HE SOLVE THE FAMILY PROBLEM?

Our Lord is the restorer of the family. The way to restore a brother and sister's family is the only way to approach a fundamental problem. The problem of Lazarus' family began with death. Because my brother is dead, my sister will be in great sorrow. Then the way to overcome the problem is to solve death. The sister knew well about the resurrection. In conversation with the Lord, I believe my brother will live again on the last day. He says. But the sisters did not think about the Lord's ability to overcome death and bring it back to life.

The important thing is now. Martha's words are not wrong, but the important thing is to believe in the Lord who lives now. We must believe in the Lord, who can now give to a home without hope a living hope of eternity, a living hope of resurrection.

The Lord says to take away the great stone that is in front of the tomb. The reason for relocating the stone is obvious evidence that Lazarus apparently died and was buried. It is a visual indication that you are already dead and buried. It is the most dramatic moment.

The Lord calls the name of Lazarus in a loud voice before the tomb. "Come out of Lazarus!" Before he raised Lazarus, the Lord prayed. The content of that prayer is thankful to God who will listen to his prayers in verses 41, 42. And every time he always prays, he is sure of God who listens to prayer. And he thinks of God first. This caused many to recall Lazarus from death when he saw the time of returning to God with the hope of resurrection. It is not until a few days after the death of the resurrection event that will happen in the distant future that it arose in front of many people.

In the Lord's call, Lazarus walked out of the tomb himself with a towel on his face while keeping his limbs in place. His body was in incorruption and in a glorious resurrection body. And he told her to let him go. This word has a symbolic meaning. We were all in the grave of sin before we received Jesus. And we were rotting in sin. One day, however, he was evangelized and received the call of the Lord. And we believe in Jesus. We did not believe but we heard the Lord's command and believed.

It is to release the wraps around the body. It is to remove the vice. The rope of sin, the rope of death that binds the whole body, and the rope of despair have reached all to the end. Lazarus came out of the grave but is still in vain. You have to take off the vet. We must remove the vengeance of the authority of death. And you have to go.

We should enjoy being free in our faith. The Lord does not want us to be good in our souls. I want to be free from everything, to be better, and to be healthier. If like veterinary issues, such as a rope that tie the body, still cover the home, it should be solved with a victory of faith with the hope of resurrection.

British hymn composer William Harper was emotionally weak from his youth. His health was weak. When his mother died at the age of six, he was shocked and depressed all his life. He made a suicide prayer several times. However, when he read the Bible, he became convinced of the Atonement of the Blood of the Lord and became faithful to his health. He always prayed hard to live in the love of God. He overcame all anxiety, and his face shone like the sun at the time of his death, saying, I am finally in the kingdom of God now. His hymn was 190 integrated hymns. In the hymn, we are well acquainted with his belief in liberty.

"Blood like the spring water is Immanuel blood. I will cleanse this sin when I wash my sins. He repented of thy patience and washed in this fountain. I want to wash away this sinful body too. The people who have been deified will have eternal life. There is no fountain of blood in the fountain. I have a love for you."

{Meditation Point}

1)Have you ever had a crisis in your home? What is your mind toward your family?
2)Do you have faith in resurrection?

CHAPTER 30

A PERSON WHO BE CURED

Luke 17: 11-19

"Was no one found to return and give praise to God except this foreigner? Then he said to him, Rise and go; your faith has made you well. (Luke 17:18-19)"

THE CHURCH is a community. It is not a place where one person is gathered, but where many people gather together to live a faith life.

In Romans, they quoted the fact that they gave meaning to the very inner church that Paul was pointing to, the inward church in which the Holy Spirit exists in our heart.

The Bible not only emphasizes the church as a community, but it also emphasizes the intrinsic church as the Holy Spirit. It is premature to conclude in advance what should be right and proceeded. It is important to know that the church has the meaning of coincidence, that is, the gathering of believers together. It is not alone, but united. The deep meaning of the union must first be in the grace of the Lord. Without grace, the meaning of unity is meaningless. It means that only those who know grace can unite and form a community. The Lord emphasizes the faith of a person who has received grace. And he declares salvation to him. The people are not scattered. Those who are united together must be people. However, these people are not those who do not know the grace, but those who have already entered the world of grace and know spiritual joy.

LET'S LOOK AT THE BACKGROUND OF THE TEXT AND WHAT IT MEANS IN EACH SCENE.

Jesus was passing between Samaria and Galilee. He went into a village, and ten lepers were gathered to Jesus at once. They can not go near Jesus, but stand in the distance and call out Jesus' name in a loud voice. Why could not they go near Jesus and grab his garments? This was because of the law that the Jews had made so that the unclean could not go near the clean. The snare of the law was holding on to the poor. The wrong law must be remedied, but the law is not fixed, and if they want to go to the Lord, they can not get close. And ten lepers had a massive burden because they did not want to show their ugliness to others. Because of their shame, past things remained intact they left the law and built a wall. The walls they had to overcome were 'law' and 'self'.

It is the work of man that God made the law, but strengthened it, and kept it from oppressing the powerless people and leading them to the true faith. Religious leaders and priests have forgotten the basic spirit of the law God has spoken the spirit of love. It is used as a means to condemn and judge a person by the law rather than ignoring the basic spirit of loving God and loving people down, setting the law, and adding various flesh to it. The law guarantees sanctification and separation, but the true distinction comes not from the law, but from love. It is power and power to love, to think and to love for people.

If we do not love people first, our faith becomes vain faith. Faith for oneself, unreliable faith lacking love like a ringing hover, is a vain faith that has nothing to do with God.

These people condemn and criticize people. He is unable to tolerate the saints and is filled with compassion for oneself. They are all legalists. God is love, the formalists who do not know the meaning of neighbor's love.

The next barrier to lepers is their own. They are ugly and shameful ones. What do people think of me? They are always conscious of others. Would not persons criticize to me? Would not they point out that you did not keep your own body and your family properly? It is full of thought. The more we have these thoughts, the more we fear to be in front of them.

Those who are deeply wounded are always obsessed with the sense of defeat and damage consciousness. The lepers were not alone. They were living a community with ten people together. Their reason for living in a community is to rely on each other. Because they did not deal with each other, they wanted to have comfort for each other. Those shy lepers who can not stand by the Lord are truly comforted and should be loved.

JESUS ON THE SIDE OF THE WEAK

What about us? Is not there a shame in me? It should be a person who comforts and comforts the wound.

WHAT DO THEY STAND IN THE DISTANCE AND ASK? AND WHAT HAPPENS?

Stand up and ask the Lord to be careful. Jesus hears their supplication and says, "Go and show you to the priests." To show the body is to heal according to the law. When a leprosy patient is healed, he must first go to the priest to see his better body. And before all people, they must be officially declared and recognized as being clean. So they were able to enter the world of normal people. The Lord has healed them according to the law. He did not destroy the law, but he did justice to the law. But an amazing thing happened. They did not need to go to the priest to see the road, but they were healed on the street.

There is a miracle like the one healed on the road. The fact that it was healed on the road has deep meaning to have healed before the announcement to the priest means that the Lord has held them accountable until the end. He is the one who not only spoke but also showed by action. Stand away and do not be afraid. Go to the priest. What will happen? He restored ten people. He comforted the Word, believed it, and the work of miracles arose.

When the Lord told the priests to go, their bodies were leprosy. There may have been those who thought in this state how to see the priest. But once they heard the word, they wanted to go and they were healed.

We live in touch with many situations. Unexpected things happen around us. Sometimes sickness occurs and joy comes to mind. The first thing you need to know when you are in such a situation is that you need an attitude of accepting what you have planned and will for me. Whether it is sad or joyful, we must know that there is a will of God in all of our lives. He works in harmony with things we do not know, and sometimes guides us in ways we have not thought of. The next thing is important. Ten lepers have been healed at one time, but it is important to know that it is the next big thing.

HOW MANY DID THEY THANK THE LORD FOR COMING AND HEALING?

Ten people were healed, and only one of them came and gladly gave thanks to the Lord. But he was not a Jew, but a Samaritan who the Jews despised. The Samaritan was a nation excluded from the law. The Samaritan was a people who did not have to go to the priest to show themselves. But the Samaritans were obedient to the word of the Lord and tried to show himself to the priest, and when their bodies were healed they were astonished and came back again to fell down at the feet of the Lord and give thanks. The Lord looks at his goodness and asks where the others are. Where are the nines, and come to this Gentile? The Samaritan gives glory to God. And in that place the Lord is raised up, declaring salvation that your faith has saved you. The Samaritan has been healed and is given the blessing of becoming a child of God with the power of salvation. Because of his good behavior, greater comfort and love come upon him from God. We take for granted that we have received from God. You are God, and of course it is natural to look at me.

Of course, it is natural that God gave me thought and grace. But the problem is that you take it for granted. If we receive grace that we can not handle, we must be saints who appreciate God's grace. The Lord has given me his body on the cross for me, but I must have something for the Lord. The apostle Paul always told the saints that he would pay a great debt to the Lord. And he felt this debt as a sacred burden, thanking the Lord for his grace until he was a martyr, and ministry for the church for the sake of the gospel. Why was he able to do a full ministry? That ability came out right from the audit. I was so grateful for the grace of the Lord that I was overworked and living for the glory of God.

Nine have just returned from normal healing, but this one has received God's special grace. We should not think of God's grace as general grace. Nine had that idea. They saw each other and they were healed. You were healed, and I was healed. So you have forgotten the grace you received and the same thing, and what special things you have received, and have just returned to your path. Some talk about this story in relation to the folly of the Jews. The Jews received God's marvelous grace, chosen grace, but lightly regarded the grace and did not endure grace. But those who believe in Jesus Christ have received special grace. Like a person who has been healed, he gives special meaning to his healing and gives thanks.

All non-Jewish Gentiles today should give special meaning to their salvation and thank the Lord. We must live for the glory of God. The nearest Jews have now become the greatest enemy. Christianity among Jews is said to be less than 2%. They reject Jesus. They do not believe. It has become the object of the greatest mission. They have disregarded the grace of God. We need to know how valuable I am to one person. You are the most gracious. We should not think of it as grace for everyone. You must know that He remembered me and called me. You must know that He is still holding on to me.

{Meditation Point}

1)Let's look at our faith. Do we live under the law? Do you live under the law of grace? If you do not love the saints and live for yourself, your heart is full of the laws you have made. It makes it impossible for others to bear. What about you?

2)Have you ever met anything unexpected in my life?

3)Have I not taken lightly the grace of God? You should not treat you like any other person. You are a special person of God.

CHAPTER 31

LORD! I DESPERATELY WANT IT.

Luke 18: 35-43

"Jesus said to him, Receive your sight; your faith has healed you (Luke 18:42)."

THERE IS a physical blindness, but the Lord says to guard against spiritual blindness. What does spiritual blindness mean? They are those who have not met the Lord. Those who have not repented to possessing the kingdom of God, and those who are not born of the Spirit, are called spiritual blind. Paul says that spiritually blind men still live as servants of the flesh. The servants of the flesh are slaves of sin, and they live according to the desires of the flesh. Those who live without pursuing the values of the kingdom of God, looking at the rotting of this earth and pursuing them as if they were their own lives. Jesus tells us to guard against spiritual blindness. Today, the people should not lose their important value because of their spiritual closeness, their anxieties. What should the people do? They are not the subjects of salvation. People can not save themselves and can not save others. The people are also objects of salvation. The Lord tells us not to be spiritual blind to us. Spiritual blindness can lead others to the wrong path.

Physical blindness can not see the front, but instead of seeing the front, the other physical senses are highly developed. God is just. He finds out what I do not have from others. And let others know what I have, and let them share their weaknesses. If they do not share their own things, then they too will be taken as sins. The Lord is working together rather than working alone. It is a great blessing for the saints to be able to enjoy a fair life for everyone. So what we have to do first is to share it and share it with one another. There is a desire to share. The desire to have only one's own is not a true wish but a desire based on vain greed. I desperately want to know that the wish is not only for me but for others as well.

WHO WAS BARTIMAEUS AND WHAT KIND OF LIFE DID HE LIVE IN?

In the text, Bartimaeus is said to be sitting on the roadside and begging. He was the son of DiMeo (Mark 10:46). We do not specifically mention DiMeO. Only Bartimaeus had a family. Israel was a family-centered society. As in the old society, there was a clear order among the families, and in some households, some people lived together in a family. Bartimaeus would surely have had such a family. However, the present situation of Bartimaeus was to keep alive while begging others. If his family were neither materially rich nor had any problems in the family, he would have to live comfortably without having to beg. Bardimaeus was in charge of the family life while begging him. He would have tried to do all alone. If he could see everything, it would not be a problem.

I know that there are a lot of people living this life living around. When I have to do all the work of my family alone, and when I have to solve all things by myself without helping anyone, I have a lonely thought, and sometimes I feel sad.

In the Gospel of Matthew, Bartimaeus notes that he was on the roadside with his other friends. That's why Bartimaeus needed a man who was willing to depend on his heart.

WHAT DOES BARTIMAEUS HEAR? AND WHAT DOES HE DO?

Suddenly there was a sound of the crowds when he was sitting on the roadside. "He is Jesus of Nazareth." "He came to Jericho."
Instead of seeing the Bartimaeus, hearing, smell, and tactile senses were developed. He heard the word of Jesus of Nazareth among the noisy crowds. At the moment, he intuitively finds out that Jesus, who had been only hearing from rumors, visited Jericho.

Bartimaeus had much interest in his current situation. What was his problem? And he knew what he needed. Those who ask God and pray to God need to know first. Why do I pray that I should go before God? You need to know if you should. You can not come to Him without looking at your problems. Christians are those who have a clear purpose. God leads Christians according to God's purpose and according to their vision. The important thing is that my vision and God's heart must match. If I have a clear plan, I must ask God before I have a wish. You should not cover your problems. When we actively ask and knock on the door, God opens and shows us the way. Bartimaeus did not hesitate. When the opportunity came, this time was the time and thought and went out to the party of Jesus. He screamed. Bartimaeus was not conscious of them when they ignored the blind, saying that others were noisy and disturbing. Only the word of Jesus of Nazareth came to his ears. For Bartimaeus, the goal of life was to meet Jesus. If you are the one who heals and heals you as you really have heard, I was sure that you would trust your own problems, and then you were ready for that. When you prepare and wait, the time will come.

WHY IS HE IN THE TEXT? DID HE CALL JESUS "THE SON OF DAVID"?

Bartimaeus had no eyes, but spiritual eyes were open. He could not see the miracle he had ever seen. If he could see, he could have believed it more easily, but he could not see the scene of such a miracle because he could not see it. Nevertheless, Bartimaeus believed that Jesus was the son of David. Why? It is because you have heard right in your ear and have developed faith. Jesus blessed those who did not see and believed. Now, many evangelists who proclaim and proclaim the Word will testify with their mouths. And blessed are those who hear and believe in the word which is proclaimed in their lips. It means. Bartimaeus' faith is good because he did not see it, but hearing and believing in his ear.

True faith is the true faith that sees what is invisible. People continue to ban Bartimaeus. Nevertheless, Bartimaeus lamented the Lord many times in the loud voice, saying, "Son of David." "Son of David has mercy on me!" "Son of David, look at me one time!" In this word, Bartimaeus' desperate mind is put into it. It is filled with a spiritual desire. Jesus heard the voice of his desperate heart. Even if many people do sanctions, the Lord has told them to leave it alone. Here we know the heart of the Lord.

The Lord had never seen Bartimaeus, but he acknowledged the zeal of

Bartimaeus. A desperate mind that could not give up moved the heart of the Lord.

There was a person who prayed, no matter when or where he got time, and he prayed with a sincere heart every time he prayed. He asked him how much of his sincere desire, and he said that he would pray with such desperate feelings that he would struggle to keep his trunk and not fall down to live on the edge of the cliff. We have all experienced such desperate feelings. There will be no one who has not experienced such a desperate feeling that so many difficulties in life are so breathtaking as to really tie up our necks.

The problem is that the prayer comes when it comes to its desperate feelings, and if even a little life becomes peaceful and the shadow of the problem is lifted a little, the desperate feeling will disappear naturally. When I am desperate, prayer comes out, and when that moment passes, it becomes a sense of when it is done.

Praying is restoring a desperate feeling every moment of prayer. That prayer should be made to God with desperate desire. There is no content of formal prayer content. It is a prayer that you just put out time. Such prayer can not move the mind of God and make one united. Prayer does not depend on the amount or time of prayer. It is not a good prayer because you pray long and many times.

Bartimaeus only repeated a word. Son of David, have mercy on me. This short statement contains all his confessions of faith. The Son of David is the acknowledgment of what God is. It is God-centered prayer. And ask me to have mercy on me. It is to look at his situation. This short prayer contains everything.

A good prayer was completed in his eager attitude. Jesus called him up. At first, people disagreed and ignored the Bartimaeus, but because they were so eager to ask, the short prayer moved the hearts of the people and made people feel relieved. "He calls you. Get up in peace. He calls you." Bartimaeus ran out of his coat all over the ground. Jesus asks him, "What do you want me to do for you?" The first coming Bartimaeus was the one who could not see. This one can not see the way. Then we can guess the reason that came before the Lord. The reason he came out because he is a blind person is that he should look ahead. Yet the Lord himself asked. Though you already knew, he asked him again. To confirm his prayer title again. Once again, Bartimaeus invariably says his wishes.

"Lord, I want to see." He listened to the word and said, "Go, your faith has saved you." He did not give him an ordained hand. He just fixed it with a word. This means the ability of prayer. The actions of faith in Bartimaeus have made it possible for them to heal themselves.

As Bartimaeus opens his eyes to faith, all people glorify and praise God. His behavior is beneficial to all and has a good influence. Even if only one person is praying, it means that the family lives and the church stand right.

> "If you have faith, you will receive whatever you pray for."
> (Matthew 21:22)

{Meditation Point}

1)Have you ever felt lonely in your life? I want you to look back on our lives to see if I had to bear all the crucifixes to bear.
2)How much preparation and wait did I spend to hear the Lord's answer?

CHAPTER 32

LET THE FIG TREE DRY

Mark 11: 12-24, 20-25

"Therefore I tell you, whatever you ask for in prayer, believe that you have received it and it will be yours (Mark 11:24)."

JESUS OFTEN spoke against the fig tree in the Word. The fruitless fig tree from the parable has a different meaning from the text. A fig tree without fruit means that the Lord waits forever until the judgment.

This means that God will give more time and opportunity to repentance until the person who is to be judged again repents and turns back from the sin and corrects his deeds. And yet another tree of figs is a fruit that can not bear fruit, so it is like a shell, and in the end, there is nothing to reap, meaning that you will be judged.

And here he goes further and sees the fig tree without fruit today, and realizes that he is lamenting the unbelieving generation, the age of this distrust that it does not ask the Lord.

It is said that they live in the age of distrust. In other words, it means compassion for a generation without faith. No one cares about the Lord. Western Christianity accepted earlier than the Eastern. Christian civilization began to blooms from the West. Numerous churches were built, theology established, and faith reformed but what about this age?

The countries that accepted the past gospel are challenged by the developed civilization and the faith of the people is shaking.

The church in Europe is empty, and it is giving place to the great challenge of atheism. It can be said that this age is the time of distrust. An example is an age when no one listens to the word of the Lord and the rarity of the word that can only be heard in the church or in the future. This is the time when the fruitless tree, the faith, was absent.

WHEN DID HE SHOW THIS MIRACLE AND WHERE IS THE BACKGROUND?

It happened in Bethany. When he came to the area, Jesus was hungry. He could not eat and he was exhausted by a long trip.

But he saw a fig tree far away. Jesus went to the side of the tree, but could not find anything because at that time the fig fruit was not opened. Nevertheless, Jesus cursed the fig tree.

"From now on, the fig tree will dry up," he said, "no man will eat from you any fruit forever." And the Lord says: I tell you the truth, if you have faith and do not doubt not only can you do what was done to the fig tree, but also you can say to this mountain, go throw yourself into the sea, and it will be done(Matthew 21: 21).

When did this miracle happen? It is morning. The Lord was active early in the morning. It speaks strongly of the personality of Jesus. He was hungry because he was a human, and he had the same feelings. We find out some facts that are hard to understand for ordinary people like the following.

IT IS A MIRACLE FOR ONESELF AND THIS GENERATION.

In every ministry of miracles, the Lord has always been more interested in others than in himself and knows that he has helped them. He thought more about others first than himself. The event of turning water into wine is also a miracle for all who came to the feast. And there were many miracles, such as miracles that made fish for Peter, and miracles that opened eyes for the blind. But if you look at the miracle of letting the fig tree dry, it is quite different from the Lord's intention. This miracle is a miracle mixed with feelings because you can not eat, you have cursed. The Lord was hungry, and the disciples did not get the fruit they desired, so they would dry up.

IT WAS NOT THE TIME TO OBTAIN THE FIG FRUIT AT THAT TIME.

Jesus, who is from Israel, would have known the natural environment better than anything else. Because he lived for over thirty years, he would know when plants grow and get fruit. The figs of Israel only bear fruit in September. But this is April. It was an unexpected time. It is like being annoyed that there are no strawberries in winter. It is natural that it is not opened, but the Lord cursed that fig tree.

From root

The tree begins to drift from the leaves and to have the disease. Sometimes they are dead from their roots, but most trees come down from the leaves with the disease. It is natural that the tree is dried leaves. But as soon as he cursed, it was dried from the roots. What does this mean? Drying from the root means complete judgment. The only thing that he said was that the tree had been cut off from its roots and its life was blocked. It is strange that the Lord's will is a rich fruit, which he purposefully dried up. The Lord's miracle has always had a positive effect. However, this miracle has a rather negative effect. It was hard for people to understand the Lord's actions, and cursing the wrong fig tree without error was another Lord's action.

LET'S THINK ABOUT THE LORD'S INTENTIONS.

The Lord judges a man who boasts only a leafless leaf without fruit. This is similar to the fruitless fig tree, as learned from the parable. But if you look for a deeper meaning than that analogy, you mean that the Lord is far from the glorious ones without a fruit. The Pharisees and scribes could not bear the fruit God wanted in their lives, but they paid attention only to what they showed on the surface. After all, their faith has become a hypocritical (pretended) faith like an empty shell. It is like the religious zeal which only points out their actions. If salt does not serve as a salty function, it is useless.

A leafless tree is a faith without action, a mouth full of words, a rotten well that did not get water, an unresponsive prayer, a false love without true love. Pastor Oswald Smith, Pastor of the America Peoples Church, Canada's largest church, says this prayer. "I want to be a minister who is more in the heart of the Lord." I want to be worthy of the will of the Lord rather than honor. It was a prayer. As a result, he was used as a good pastor to send and help hundreds of missionaries.

The word has power.

The Lord cursed only with his mouth. But it has dried up from its roots. It is not dried from the leaves but dried from the roots. What does this mean? I know that one word has the ability to die and to live. The word has power and works as it is. It is said that the thread we use easily comes from the silkworm. However, the thread comes out of the mouth of the silkworm. The length is 300 meters. The silk wraps the silkworm. Likewise, words from our mouth surround us and make us human. Isaac was blessed through words. Isaac asks the Father when he goes up mount Moriah to offer Isaac a burnt offering. Where is the sheep for burnt offerings? But Abraham was prepared by God. It is said. Isaac and Abraham understood and accepted different meanings, but they were literally accomplished.

The most powerful language is prayer.

What the Lord has said has been done, and He teaches us to pray. "Believe in what you have prayed for and received what you asked for." This means the ability of prayer. It is the ability of prayer that a fig tree dries up. Prayer enables impossible things, and prayer provides the power to overcome reality, not to escape reality. Therefore, the Lord teaches that he who dried up the fig tree also came out of prayer. The fig tree is just a creation. The fig tree is only a tree. It can be said that God, the Creator, used the creature of figs to teach the lesson to man. Think about it. Would you curse that man against a fig tree? Because it is a tree, he has done miracles to teach lessons.

He teaches that not only prayer but also faith is important.

Faith drives the throne of God. What dried up from the roots means that work will happen in everything that is done by faith?

It appears when we believe in God's power without making any limits. The meaning hidden in faith is 'Dynamite'. It is faith that exerts an explosive power. Imagine that this faith comes together in many people, not in one person. Imagine that dynamite is made up of several bundles instead of one. The power is beyond imagination. A person's faith is important, but it is also important to have a faith together and a faith to join together.

Proper prayer and faith break the formal life of faith.

The prayers of faith make one another. They can exert great ability and unite each other. If we say that there is faith, and prayerfulness does not break the community or prevent us from becoming one, his faith and prayer end up in a formal sense that is not for himself or for the community at all.

The Lord speaks. "When you stand and pray, if you have any doubt, forgive. And your Father who is in heaven will also forgive your transgressions." Standing and praying is going to pray in the open. Pray on behalf of others. Everyone sees the life of a person standing and praying. But what happens to those who stand and listen to the prayer if they can not practice the Word themselves and love them? No one will try to hear the prayer. Those who stand and pray should first show forgiveness and love. Then God hears the prayer, and forgives all transgressions.

In order to receive God's forgiveness, we must first show how we forgive our brothers. The reason we let the fig tree dry is that it means the Lord's teaching that we should not live a leafy life, that we should pray for faith as a true believer, and that we should live together in unity with one another.

{Meditation Point}

1)Did you live a life of faithful prayer? How much did you forgive and love your brother?

CHAPTER 33

BEAR THIS!

Luke 22: 47-53

"But Jesus answered, No more of this! And he touched the man's ear and healed him (Luke 22:51)."

IT IS a true story from any overseas news. A 34-year-old man decided to avenge his wife who had abandoned him and broke a bomb at her wedding party, killing 36 people and injuring 30 others. The man, formerly a bomb expert, died on the spot when he rushed to the wedding ceremony with a 50kg bomb on the day. It was the worst event that caused the anger and jealousy which had abandoned oneself and took away even the child. But it was when the wife and three children had not arrived at the place yet.

In the end, it was a sad case that innocent men and women lost their life because he could not control his feelings of anger. Large and small events occur a lot around us. According to the data released by the National Police Agency during the past 10 years, most of the incidents were caused by the inability to control the emotions. I can not control my own person, I can not bear anger, and I express it to others. Sometimes it is violent for people to look at the road. Due to the influence of the mass media, children or youth are increasingly violent. Especially teenage crime is becoming increasingly cruel.

The problem is that they do not feel any remorse and do not feel sorry for the victim. If adults do not control their own feelings, they will eventually do something irreversible. Christians should be able to control their emotions. People often get angry. And we live with angry feelings. But it is important to rule it. Failure to control the wrath at home in the church will ultimately damage the Church of God and destroy precious homes. In today's Word, the Lord tells his disciples to rule over his feelings.

The main contents and events of the story are that Judas arrived at the Mount of Olives to accuse Jesus with the crowd, and that Peter wielded a sword to stop it, and that the ear of the servant of high priest was injured in the process, and that the Lord warned Peter, It is the case that fixed it.

WHAT HAPPENS AFTER PRAYER? WHAT IS THE RESPONSE OF THE DISCIPLES AND WHAT DOES THE LORD SAY TO THEM?

Those who stirred up the Jewish people were just religious leaders for the people still listened diligently when the Lord taught them in the temple. But the leaders hated the Lord and tried to kill him. (19: 47-48; 21: 37-22: 2). Luke pointed out that Jesus had more responsibility for the sufferings of the leaders than the people. What is the position of the leader? It is the role of leading the people in the right way. But they did not, and rather they inspired the people to hate each other. Peter was the one who was most affected by emotions. He had a character that could not bear injustice. It was a character that would surely fix if there was something wrong.

What happened in front of the eyes was unfair. Even though there was no sin, the leaders were going to take the Lord. Peter, who had no patience before the injustice, pulled out a sword and pointed at the high priest, but cut off the ears of a slave who had no fault. The ears were cut off and blood began to appear. The Lord stopped Peter and said, "Hold on until now!" And rightly touching the ears of Malgo, a miracle of clean healing arises.

The Lord did not give over to those who were in trouble first even in the unfortunate circumstances of being betrayed and drawn away. What does this mean?

There is a symbolic meaning for the suffering and death of the Lord. He is the one who is arrested and saved through death.

WHAT DO WE NEED TO REALIZE THROUGH THE INCIDENT?

Here we must be a lesson, seeing the foolish actions of Peter and his disciples.

First, it is the difference between praying and not doing. Look at the Lord! He prayed earnestly in front of the Father before death. We can find the example that there will be a prayer for every verse. There is a scene in which the Lord asks and the Lord prayed directly. The Lord encourages Peter to continue to pray, but Peter hears it only in his ears and flows away. He falls asleep because he can not overcome the lust of the body.

He did not pray, and when he reached a dangerous environment, he lived on his own disposition. If you do not pray well, your old temperament is likely to come alive again. If you do not pray, you will have weakness in your test and less spiritual attention. It is easy to live according to emotion, and it does not control the mind. This phenomenon appears to Peter who does not pray.

Second, you should not be overconfident with yourself. Peter once confessed to the Lord, "You are the Christ, the Son of the living God." And he said I will never betray you even if everyone betrays you. But Peter was easily betrayed the night the Lord was captured. This is because he was so convinced of himself. He promised he would not. However, they easily succumb to the environment. He knew the Lord only as the Son of God. Peter did not know that the Lord had to die on the cross to redeem as the Son of God. The crucifixion of the cross is part of God's plan. The Lord has obeyed the will of this God and has given his life. We think I know everything. But it is not. The same is true of the spiritual world. In the deep and amazing spiritual world, there are many things we still do not know. If Peter knew that the Lord would be taken away and be resurrected, there would have been no reason to put his ears in the ears. It is the heart of a person who hears only one of the words. A true Christian is one who knows many things through one. And they are always those who think and prepare on the side of the Lord.

Third, Malgo is just a servant. He has no power. He came only as a worker of the high priest, but Peter hurt his ear. It is so stupid to try to reign over the weak. The Lord always stands on the side of the weak. It is on the side of those who are marginalized, exploited, and servants of sin. He lives as a laborer of God.

It is God's character that tells us what He has done to heal. He leads me from a failed life to a successful life. The Lord is their friend when they are despised that they have nothing to live, that they have no status in the world. There are many who are not in us. How has the life of Malgo changed after hearing his ears? He may not have been present in the Bible, but perhaps he had experienced miracles and later became a disciple of Christ, living the life of an evangelist who testified of what had happened to him and witnessed the gospel. Just as all the characters of the Bible lived like that. It is a great blessing for those who have been living with the Lord at first to have changed and are now living as faithful servants of the Lord.

Fourth, we must know the Lord's heart. The disciples became one with the lust for the Lord. When he told them to pray, they were not one, but when they used to force each other, they had a heart. Will Peter take up the sword and the other disciples will also be swords? They will ask. It was not the Lord's thrill but the Lord's rebuke that came to them.

Matthew 26:52 put your sword back on the road. Every man with a sword is ruined by a sword. The word means that Jesus does not accomplish work by force. It can not be justified for any purpose, whether it is for good or for power. The violence raises violence, and hate brings another hate. Eventually, everything is destroyed. It is only a vicious cycle.

Do you know that I can not ask the Father to send an angel who is twelve more army now? Do you know that I am caught by them because I have no strength? This means that the Lord can use the power of angels at any time, but not because of lack of strength, but to teach that the Lord's path is the way of the cross. We must be saints who act according to the will of the Lord. The zeal that is not related to the will of the Lord has nothing to do with the Lord.

Where we live is a world of injustice. Most of the articles on the internet site appeal to the public about the almost unfairness. As I live, I get a lot of bad things. And there are so many people in the world who live in unfair work, so that there is a "group of people who have been treated unfairly" on the Internet. When you enter the world, there are a lot of unfair events coming out of the story. A woman walked down the street and was struck by a taxi that rushed into India and died on the spot. But she can not get a reward. How unlucky is this? The reason for this is that the taxi driver is not responsible and the passenger who is drunk in the taxi is wrong, he was assaulting the driver while drunk, and suddenly he mishandled the steering wheel.

An innocent citizen died. There are a lot of people in this world who are subjected to such unfair work and suffer losses. The Bible tells us that it is the Lord who repays the grudge. Only God knows my circumstances. The Bible tells us that we should have the will to give thanks to Him who knows all about me, and not to repay evil for evil, but for good.

The Word of the Lord says not to prepare swords for blood and flesh, but to prepare swords in spiritual fighting. (Ephesians 6:12) The object of the battle is not man. The object of our struggle is the evil spirit. It is Satan. In order to win the spiritual battle, the emotions should abstain from minor things and the evil should not be repaid as evil. The Lord says to us, "Be patient!" In order to win the spiritual battle, I need to know what I have to endure now.

If I really love the Lord, if I want to confess that I love Jesus just like Peter, I will "endure to this end, as the Lord has said" (you know what this is). I hope you will realize that I am the blessed way to follow Him.

{Meditation Point}

1)The enemy we fight is not on the outside but inside. The Lord has triumphant in prayer in his struggle with himself. The disciples, however, fail in prayer and lose their inner and enemy fights first.

CHAPTER 34

INVITAITON OF JESUS

John 21: 1-14

"Jesus said to them, come and have breakfast. None of the disciples dared ask him, who are you? They knew it was the Lord (John 21:12)."

THOSE WHO have not experienced defeat in life can not expect internal growth and maturity. The resurrection faith is the faith of surviving again. It is the faith to stand up for the environment in a situation that is irreversible. The Lord wants Christians to live not only on the cross but also on the resurrection faith. So, after he had lived again, the Lord had visited the beaches of Tiberias in search of his disciples who had been obsessed with the emotion of defeat. God has come for those who have been defeated.

Everyone is living frustrated once in a while. There will be no one who has not felt frustration or loss. Humanity has begun tragic life from severe frustration. Adam and Eve were driven out of the Garden of Eden with a sense of frustration that they could not keep the word of God. When we think about the situation of the two, it tells us what frustration we are feeling today. There was no shortage in the garden. Everything was perfect. They did not have to feel the despair from eating and living. The life itself under God's law was a satisfying life that God guaranteed and led life. However, the life outside of God's control was itself a continuation of despair.

Adam had a sense of accomplishment and disillusionment from unparalleled poverty in his lifetime of work, and Eve had to suffer the most extreme trials of humanity from the suffering of the parturition. What about his children Cain and Abel? Cain compares with his brother before God, feeling extreme frustration, and even capturing himself in the losing consciousness of his brother, which eventually led to the stigma of mankind's first killer to kill his brother. This is the beginning of mankind. People live with deep frustration and feelings of defeat. Everyone here has no exceptions. In this situation, God creates a bridge for those in decline to escape from the valley of despair to overcome defeat and frustration. The Lord knows all those who are in despair easily. Because the Lord is the Creator, knows all the processes of human crime, and why can they be despairing and frustrated? You know why. The Lord often comes to those who are lost. Today's message also came to disciples who had accumulated in the defeat, and came to disciples to solve the desperation as a result of human fundamental sin.

WHO CAME FIRST ON THE BEACH OF TIBERIAS? WHY DID THEY GO TO THE SEA AND WHAT DID THEY DO THERE?

For the first time, Tiberias, where the disciples were looking for, was the place where those who had experienced failure met. On the beach of Tiberias where Jesus came, it was the place where people who had tasted great frustration in life gathered.

The common feature of people who have experienced failure once is that they are away from their lives for a while. Those who have experienced failure to do business do not want to go back to the scene of failure. So they take off for a while and then they go back to the original place they were after taking the rest of their mind and started a new start in a whole new place. Tiberias beach was such a place for the disciples. When the Lord died, the disciples were not in the field of crucifixion. They were not in the place before the Lord was captured. Because of the deep disappointment and frustration, it took place for a while and gathered to the beach. On the shore of Tiberias were Simon Peter and Thomas named Diumotho, Nathanael the Galanaite, and the sons of Zebedee, and two other disciples? They were now mentally shocked. It is in a panic state.

If you are shocked, you will not be able to do anything. What to do? I do not know well. The one who has so relied on is dead now, and there is no one beside him. Who has relied on them for many years to lead them, but because they are reluctant to do so, they think that everything is desperate and that they have been defeated in their lives. So Peter remembers his past career. What I can do right now is catching fish. It was the thing that I remembered and learned about my past as a fisherman. So Peter went out to the seashore, "I am going to catch fish." Peter was a fisherman, and two other brothers were fishermen in the past. But now that he has spoken, all the other disciples are willing to follow Peter. Thomas, and Nathanael, and they also followed him, saying that Peter would go. This indicates that their mental state is almost abandoned. They knew that they had nothing to do, and they followed Peter.

It was a great sadness to lose the beloved Lord, and their act of fleeing before their teacher's death was embarrassing, and now fear of livelihood has begun to dominate the mind. All the disciples thought they were losers.

He went to Peter, who was going to catch fish without any purpose to overcome the sense of defeat. But what was the result? He was on a boat but could not catch anything tonight. He tried to get fish even though he had a feeling of comfort, but there was a big sense of loss that he could not catch even when he gave up everything.

WHY DID NOT THEY CATCH ANYTHING?

They could not catch anything. The special lesson they learned is that you can do nothing with your own strength. What they need is only the risen Lord, to know Him, and to meet Him personally. And that they can not be self-sufficient by their own strengths. The lives of disciples who are not in the Lord were less and the uneasy life lasted. Jesus took the experiences of those who could not hold anything and made them his opportunity to teach them again that He is the risen Lord. Sometimes the Lord works for us. He drives us to the corner of life so that we must receive Him.

Though they thought that they could live well without the Lord, it is their idea that there is nothing that can be done without the Lord from those who have already experienced the graced and spiritual world. This is the most important time. People tend to drive to the extremes if they are not always available. It is important to realize that a small thing becomes a big thing and there is a lot of cost later. I am already abandoned, so let's live happily. It is the idea that it should be discarded. When it is not the first time, it should be overcome well. You have to overcome. The disciples were not long in despair because the Lord came to them.

WHAT DID THE LORD COME TO HIS DISCIPLES AND WHAT DID HE DO? LET US CONSIDER THE WILL OF GOD.

Now Tiberias is no longer a place of failure, but a place of departure for a new ministry. The life of the disciples is blessed with the encounter of Jesus of the Lord.

When the night was not catching fish, the Lord came to them at dawn and said, "Throw the net on the right side. Then you will get what you want." This statement has the same meaning as saying "go down into the deep and throw the net" when he called Peter. Going deeper and throwing the net means Jesus' first intervention in Peter's life. In the past, Peter alone. The Lord came to him who was thirsty in a lonely and spiritual world and told him to comfort Peter's broken heart. It is the same meaning that He came to the woman in the land of Samaria and asked for a glass of water. The Lord does not just come to us. It comes amidst the problems I face. "What is your problem?" "Do not worry alone, bring it to me." Throw on the right side of the boat. Then you will get the answers you want. To bring down the net contains the great love of the Lord who invites his disciples into the world of His grace.

The disciples obeyed the word and sent down their nets. And when John, the beloved disciple of Jesus, heard that he was the Lord to Peter, he marched in the cloak and received Him. As we studied the last time, John was the disciple who was with the Lord until the end. So he knew that he was Lord. The Lord had already prepared everything on the land. The disciples, who had worked hard to get through the night but could not get anything, were now trembling with hunger and cold. When they came up to them, they were all ready to eat. And what did they say to them? "Come and have breakfast." Come and prepare for breakfast and eat. Jesus took the bread directly and gave it to them, and they also gave him fish. He cooked his own food and fed his disciples. It was disheartened disciples. There was a transgression that betrayed the Lord, and a transgression that fled and fled from him, and all this was acceptable, and the Lord himself gave food to his disciples. Jesus is living God who can prepare everything for his chosen people. He is the one who knows everything and has prepared everything.

A ministry without love is nothing!

For Christians, the beautiful encounter between the Lord and his disciples makes many things happen. There is one great lesson here. Love is an essential element of ministry. These ministries lacking love, advice without love are of no value to God. Because he loved his disciples, he did not forget them and he was looking for them again. What about people? Easily turn around and betray. I am good at the front, but when I look back, I am remorseful when I do it. The most variable is the mind of a person. The disciples did. But the Lord did not. The disciples were weak and easily changed, but the Lord loved them. Because he was in love, he came directly to the beach. And he prepares the defeated life to rise again and restores the broken relationship.

{Meditation Point}

1)Did I ever think that I was a loser? Have you ever experienced a greater sense of loss that you are giving up everything like disciples?
2)When he called us, he called us to use it as disciples with a loving heart. I wish you and me to hear the voice of the calling of the Lord who has endured, embraced and prepared everything for us to the end. Hallelujah!

ACKNOWLEDGEMENT

THIS BOOK IS WRITTEN FOR THE WEAK AND THEIR MISSION OF NORTH AMERICA. JESUS ALWAYS STOOD ON THE SIDE OF THE WEAK PEOPLE OF THE EARTH AND PREACHED THE JUSTICE OF GOD AND HIS KINGDOM. ESPECIALLY I WOULD LIKE TO EXPRESS MY SINCERE THANKS TO ALL THE DIRECTORS, PASTOR PARK JONG IK, CHOI SUN HWA, CHO JIN HEUI OF THE LIVING BREATH (SOOM) MISSION SOCIETY THAT PRAYED FOR THE MINISTRIES.

ABOUT THE AUTHOR

Yongjea John Han majored in Law and English Literature, majoring in theology in the Netherlands and the United States and Honam Presbyterian Theological Seminary. He also worked as a poet and writer in Korea. He then moved to Canada to continue his work as a writer and missionary. He and his wife and two children, near Chilliwack, BC, are dedicated to a mission for the weak and writing activities.

[Books: *Slow City, The Space, Refugees, The Old Memories of Tynehead, The Qs about the Alists, Refugees Ali, Jesus On the side of the Weak*]

www.ingramcontent.com/pod-product-compliance
Lightning Source LLC
LaVergne TN
LVHW011912080426
835508LV00007BA/485